James Charles Cox

A Monograph of Australian Land Shells

James Charles Cox

A Monograph of Australian Land Shells

ISBN/EAN: 9783337312350

Printed in Europe, USA, Canada, Australia, Japan

Cover: Foto ©Andreas Hilbeck / pixelio.de

More available books at **www.hansebooks.com**

MONOGRAPH
OF
AUSTRALIAN LAND SHELLS.

BY

JAMES C. COX, M.D., Univ. Edin., F.R.C.S. Edin.

CORRESPONDING MEMBER OF THE ZOOLOGICAL SOCIETY OF LONDON.
CORRESPONDENT OF THE ACADEMY OF NATURAL SCIENCES OF PHILADELPHIA,
U.S. AMERICA. MEMBER OF ROYAL MEDICAL SOCIETY OF EDINBURGH,
ROYAL AND ENTOMOLOGICAL SOCIETIES OF NEW SOUTH WALES.

ILLUSTRATED BY XVIII PLATES.

WILLIAM MADDOCK, 383 GEORGE STREET, SYDNEY;
GEORGE ROBERTSON, 69 ELIZABETH STREET, MELBOURNE;
GEORGE SLATER, QUEEN STREET, BRISBANE;
W. C. RIGBY, ADELAIDE;
TRÜBNER & CO., 16 PATERNOSTER ROW, LONDON.

1868.

PREFACE.

Since the publication of my Catalogue of Australian Land Shells in 1864, numerous new species have been added to the Australian Fauna described by Pfeiffer, Morelet, Adams, Angas, myself, and other authors, many of the typical species of which are in the collection of the Australian Museum, in my own, and other private collections in the Colony. To enable Conchologists to correctly distinguish the newly described species, and to prevent an accumulation of synonyms, I have undertaken to give a synopsis in this Monograph of all known Australian Land Shells, with their full descriptions; figuring as far as lies in my power all well-defined species in XVIII plates. I hope soon to be in a position to supplement these, as several new and valuable specimens have very recently been added to my collection.

For the habitats given, I am much indebted to my late friend, Mr. John MacGillivray, Mr. Masters, the Rev. R. L. King, Mr. F. A. Blackman, Mr. Blomfield, Captain Edwards, and other friends on whose authority the strictest reliance can be placed.

The Illustrations, kindly executed for me by Miss Scott and Mrs. Edward Forde, speak for themselves, and I have no doubt will be duly appreciated by the public.

JAMES C. COX., M.D.

130 *Phillip Street, Sydney,*
   New South Wales.

INDEX.

ORDERS, SUB-ORDERS, SECTIONS, FAMILIES, DISTINGUISHED BY CAPITALS; GENERA, BY SMALL CAPITALS; SPECIES, BY ROMAN LETTERS; SYNONYMS, REFERENCES, &c., BY ITALICS.

	PAGE
ACHATINELLA. *Swainson*	77
— *Achatinella. Swainson*	78
— *Bulimus. Scopoli*	78
— Buliinus Jacksonensis. *Cox*	77
— Frickella. *Pfeiffer*	78
— Jacksonensis. *Cox*	77
— Wakefieldiæ. *Cox*	78
ACICULACEA. *Pfeiffer*	92
AMPELITA. *Pfeiffer*	54
ANGASELLA. *Adams*	23
BALEA. *Prideaux*	81
— Australis. *Forbes*	81
BLANFORDIA. *Menke?*	94
— pyrrhostoma. *Cox*	95
— striatula. *Menke*	95
BULIMUS. *Scopoli*	68
— Adelaidæ. *Adams and Angas*	69
— *Adelaidæ. Adams and Angas*	69
— Angasianus. *Pfeiffer*	70
— atomatus. *Gray*	71
— Baconi. *Benson*	73
— Bidwilli. *Cox*	72
— *Bulimulus Adelaidæ. Adams and Angas*	69
— *Bulimulus lepidula. Adams and Angas*	69
— bulla. *Menke*	73
— *chrondula Adelaidæ. Adams and Angas*	69
— *chrondula lepidula. Adams and Angas*	69
— Dufresni. *Leach*	70
— *Dufresni. Leach*	73, 76
— dux. *Pfeiffer*	71
— *Helix Dufresni. Ferussac*	70
— *Helix melo. Quoy et Gaimard*	74
— *Helix melo var. Quoy et Gaimard*	74
— *Helix trilineata. Quoy et Gaimard*	75
— indutus. *Menke*	73
— *indutus. Menke*	73
— inflatus. *Lamarck*	72
— Kingi. *Gray*	75
— *Kingi. Gray*	73, 75, 76

	PAGE
BULIMUS. lepidula. *Adams and Angas*	69
— Mastersi. *Cox*	77
— melo. *Quoy et Gaimard*	74
— *melo. Quoy et Gaimard*	74, 76
— *melo var. β. Menke*	75
— Onslowi. *Cox*	74
— Pacificus. *Pfeiffer*	68
— *Pacifica. Papu. Pfr*	68
— *physoides. Reeve*	74
— Papa Ramsayi. *Cox*	69
— rhodostoma. *Gray*	76
— *rhodostoma. Gray*	73
— Sayi. *Pfeiffer*	75
— Tasmanicus. *Pfeiffer*	72
— trilineatus. *Reeve*	75, 76, 77
— Tuckeri. *Pfeiffer*	69
— Walli. *Cox*	69, 70
CALLIA. *Gray*	103
— *lubria*	104
— splendens. *Dohrn*	104
CALLICOCHLIAS. *Pfeiffer*	64
CAMÆNA. *Pfeiffer*	54
CARYODES. *Pfeiffer*	70
CONULUS. *Pfeiffer*	8
CYCLOPHOREA. *Pfeiffer*	97
CYCLOPHORUS. *Montfort*	97
— *cyclostoma liricinctum. Benson*	97
— *cyclostoma orbiculatum. Benson*	97, 98
— liricinctus	98
— liricinctus. *Reeve*	97
— *liricinctum. Reeve*	97
— orbiculatus. *Pfeiffer*	98
CYCLOSTOMACEA. *Pfeiffer*	97
CYSTICOPSIS. *Pfeiffer*	35
DERMATOCERA. H. and A. *Adams*	98
— *cyclostoma vitrea. Lesson*	98
— *Leptopoma vitreum. Lesson*	98
— vitrea. *Lesson*	98
— *vitrea. Lesson*	98
DIPLOMMATINA. *Benson*	95
— Australiæ. *Benson*	96
— Bensoni. A. *Adams*	96
DIPLOMMATINACEA. *Pfeiffer*	94
DISCUS. *Pfeiffer*	12
ECTOPHTHALMA. *Pfeiffer*	96

INDEX.

	PAGE
FRICKELLA. *Pfeiffer*	77
GALAXIAS. *Pfeiffer*	40
GEOTROCHUS. *Pfeiffer*	65
HELICIDÆ	1
HELICINA. *Lamarck*	105
— diversicolor. *Cox*	105
— Draytonensis. *Pfeiffer*	106
— Draytonensis. *Pfeiffer*	106
— fulgurata. *Cox*	107
— Gladstonensis. *Cox*	107
— Gouldiana. *Forbes*	108
— Lizardensis. *Cox*	107
— reticulata. *Pfeiffer*	106
— Yorkensis. *Pfeiffer*	108
— Yorkensis. *Pfeiffer*	107
HELICINACEA. *Pfeiffer*	105
HELICINEA. *Pfeiffer*	105
HELICOPHANTA. *Pfeiffer*	5
HELIX. *Linnæus*	1
— Adelaidæ. *Pfeiffer*	15
— albanensis. *Cox*	15
— albumenoidea. *Cox*	11
— Alexandræ. *Cox*	61
— ammonitoides. *Reeve*	18
— Angasiana. *Pfeiffer*	49
— Angasiana. *Pfeiffer*	50
— Angasiana. *Crosse*	50
— appendiculata. *Pfeiffer*	56
— appendiculata. *Pfeiffer*	55
— argillacea. *Ferussac*	43
— argillacea. *Gray*	43
— aridorum. *Cox*	44
— aridorum. *Cox* 38, 45, 60
— assimilans. *Cox* 26, 27
— atramentaria. *Shuttleworth*	5
— Australis. *Menke*	31
— Banneri. *MacGillivrayi*	6
— Belli. *Cox*	17
— Bidwilli. *Pfeiffer*	63
— bipartita. *Ferussac*	54
— bipartita. *Ferussac*	56
— bisulcata. *Pfeiffer*	32
— bitæniata. *Cox*	50
— bitæniata. *Cox*	42
— Blackmani. *Cox*	45
— Blomfieldi. *Cox*	57
— Blomfieldi. *Cox*	58
— Boivini	67
— bombycina. *Pfeiffer*	20
— Brazieri. *Cox*	14
— brevipila. *Pfeiffer*	47
— brevipila. *Pfeiffer*	48
— Bulimus Maconelli. *Reeve*	6
— bullacea. *Pfeiffer*	26
— bullacea. *Pfeiffer*	27
— Busbyi	5
— capillacea. *Ferussac*	25
— capillacea. *Ferussac* 25, 26, 28
— carcharias. *Pfeiffer*	45
— Caracolla Novæ Hollandiæ. *Gray*	68

	PAGE
HELIX. Cassandra. *Pfeiffer*	50
— cellaria.	9
— cerata. *Cox*	58
— cerata. *Cox*	58
— cerea. *Cox*	58
— circumcincta. *Cox*	3
— Clarencensis. *Cox*	4
— cochlidium. *Cox*	13
— cochlidium. *Cox*	14
— coma. *Gray*	21
— confusa. *Pfeiffer*	24
— conoidea. *Cox*	63
— conscendens. *Cox*	67
— coriaria. *Pfeiffer*	36
— coriaria. *Pfeiffer* 38, 39, 46
— corneo-virens. *Pfeiffer*	46
— corneo-virens. *Pfeiffer*	39
— corticicola. *Cox*	19
— costata. *Müller*	62
— Creedi. *Cox*. See additions
— Crotali. *Cox*	2
— cumulus. *Pfeiffer*	34
— Cunninghami. *Gray*	52
— cuprea. *Cox*	22
— Curtisiana. *Pfeiffer*	58
— cyclostoma.	16
— cyclostomata. *Le Guillou*	61
— Cygnea. *Benson*	16
— cyrtopleura. *Pfeiffer*	23
— Delessertiana. *Le Guillou*	61
— delta. *Pfeiffer*	63
— Diemenensis. *Cox*	20
— Diemenensis. *Cox* 21, 29
— Dringi. *Pfeiffer*	64
— Duclosiana. *Ferussac*	47
— ductilis. *Pfeiffer*	10
— Dunkiensis. *Forbes*	43
— Dunkiensis. *Forbes*	42
— Dupuyana. *Pfeiffer*	65
— Dupuyana. *Pfeiffer* 65, 68
— Duralensis. *Cox*	46
— Edwardsi. *Cox*. See additions
— Evandaleana. *Pfeiffer*	51
— exocarpi. *Cox*	44
— Expeditionis. *Cox*	37
— Falconari. *Reeve*	5
— Falconari. *Reeve* 6, 62
— fenestrata. *Cox*	63
— Flindersi. *Adams & Angas*	51
— Forbesi. *Cox*	58
— Forsteriana. *Pfeiffer*	42
— Franklandiensis. *Forbes*	27
— Franklandiensis. *Forbes*	30
— Fraseri. *Gray*	64
— Fraseri. *Gray* 56, 58
— fricata. *Gould*	11
— fricata Nanina. *Gould*	11
— fucata. *Pfeiffer*	67
— fucata. *Pfeiffer*	68
— funerea. *Cox*	16
— funiculata. *Pfeiffer*	46

INDEX.

	PAGE
HELIX. *funiculata. Pfeiffer*	57
— Gärtneriana. *Pfeiffer*	66
— Gärtneriana. *Pfeiffer*	67
— Georgiana. *Quoy et Gaimard*	28
— Gilberti. *Pfeiffer*	30
— Gilberti. *Pfeiffer*	36
— *glaberrima*	9
— Grandi Le. *Cox*	23
— Grayi. *Pfeiffer*	35
— Grayi. *Pfeiffer* ..36, 37, 38, 39,	42
— Greenhilli. *Cox*	40
— *gulosa. Gould*	55
— Hamiltoni. *Cox*	32
— Harriettæ. *Cox*	29
— Hobarti. *Cox*	22
— Hystrix. *Cox*	48
— *impexa. Reeve*	2
— Incei. *Pfeiffer*	54
— Incei. *Pfeiffer* 57,	58
— *inconspicua. Forbes*	2
— Indica. *Pfeiffer*	33
— inusta. *Cox*	13
— *inusta. Cox*	16
— irradiata. *Gould*	35
— iuloidea. *Forbes*	17
— *iuloidea. Forbes* .. 13, 16, 17,	23
— Jacksoniensis. *Gray*	7
— *Janellei. Le Gillou*	56
— Jervisensis. *Quoy et Gaimard*	30
— *Jervisensis. Quoy et Gaimard* 31,	36
— Kreffti. *Cox*	2
— lævsa. *Reeve*	37
— lampra. *Pfeiffer*	28
— *lampra. Pfeiffer*	29
— lamproides. *Cox*	28
— Launcestonensis. *Reeve*	31
— Le Grandi. *Cox*	23
— Leichhardti. *Cox*	25
— leptogramma. *Pfeiffer*	41
— *leptogramma. Pfeiffer*	50
— Lessoni. *Pfeiffer*	55
— *Lessoni. Pfeiffer* 55, 56,	58
— leucocheilus. *Cox*	54
— Lincolniensis. *Pfeiffer*	51
— lirata. *Cox*	15
— *lirata. Cox* 14,	20
— Lizardensis. *Pfeiffer*	33
— Lorioliana. *Crosse*	52
— luteo-fusca. *Cox*	52
— Lyndhurstensis. *Cox*	11
— MacGillivrayi. *Forbes*	62
— Macleayi. *Cox*	45
— Maconelli. *Reeve*	6
— mansueta. *Pfeiffer*	59
— *mansueta. Pfeiffer*	48
— marcescens. *Cox*	37
— *marcescens. Cox*	60
— Mariæ. *Cox*	54
— *marmorata. Cox*	3
— *Mastersi*	36
— Melbournensis. *Cox*	22

	PAGE
HELIX. microcosmos. *Cox*	3
— *microscopica. Cox*	3
— minima. *Cox*	10
— *minella. Ferussac*	3
— Mitchellæ. *Cox*	65
— monacha. *Pfeiffer*	38
— *monacha. Pfr.*	39
— Moretonensis. *Pfr.*	5
— *Moretonensis. Pfr.*	4
— morosa. *Morelet*	60
— Morti. *Cox*	21
— *Morti. Cox*	22
— mucida. *Pfr.*	59
— mucosa. *Cox*	19
— Mühlfeldtiana. *Pfr.*	53
— Mulgoæ. *Cox*	38
— murina. *Pfr.*	60
— Murphyi. *Cox*	23
— Murrayana. *Pfr.*	14
— Namoiensis. *Cox*	29
— Nanina atramentaria. *Shuttleworth*	5
— Nanina fricata. *Gould*	11
— *nautiloides. Cox*	13
— nitida. *Müller*	9
— *nitida. Müller*	7
— Novæ Hollandiæ. *Gray*	68
— *Novæ Hollandiæ, Carocolla. Gray*	68
— Omicron. *Pfr.*	18
— *Omicron. Pfr.* 18,	19
— Ophelia. *Pfr.*	34
— pachystyla. *Pfr.*	40
— *pachystyla. Pfr.* 40,	41
— pachystyloides. *Cox*	41
— *pachystyloides. Cox* 40,	45
— paleata. *Reeve*	44
— *paradora. Cox*	21
— Parramattensis. *Cox*	8
— patruelis. *Adams and Angas*	49
— *pelodes. Pfr.*	43
— Penolensis. *Cox*	8
— perinflata. *Pfr*	45
— pexa. *Cox*	13
— plectilis. *Benson*	44
— *plectilis. Benson*	64
— pliculosa. *Pfr.*	60
— Poiretiana. *Pfr.*	66
— pomum. *Pfr.*	40
— *pomum. Pfr.*	45
— Porteri. *Cox*	48
— *Porteri. Cox*	48
— prunum. *Ferussac*	43
— *prunum. Ferussac*	43
— ptycomphala. *Pfr.*	24
— *ptycomphala. Pfr.*	24
— pudibunda. *Cox*	4
— radians. *Pfr.*	7
— Ramsayi. *Cox*	30
— rapida. *Pfr.*	19
— retepora. *Cox*	21

	PAGE
HELIX. Richmondiana. *Pfeiffer*...	62
— *rotabilis*. *Reeve*	53
— rustica. *Pfr.*	2
— *rustica*. *Pfr.*	3
— Saturni. *Cox*	14
— *Saturni*. *Cox* 14, 15,	20
— Scotti. *Cox*	39
— semicastanea. *Pfr.*	56
— *seminigra*. *Crosse*	55
— sericatula. *Pfr.*	12
— *sericatula*. *Pfr.* 13,	14
— similaris. *Ferussac*	58
— similis. *Cox*	23
— Sinclairi. *Pfr.*	32
— *sphæroidea*. *Le Guillou*	40
— splendidula. *Pfr.*	10
— *splendidula*. *Pfr.*.... 27,	28
— Strangei. *Pfr.*	26
— *Strangei*. *Pfr.* 10, 25, 28,	29
— Strangeoides. *Cox*	27
— *strangulata*. *Homb. et Jacq.*	61
— Stroudensis. *Cox*	20
— Stutchburyi. *Pfr.*	39
— subangulata. *Pfr.*	12
— *subangulata*, *Adams and Angas*	3
— subgranosa. *Le Guillou*	36
— sublesta. *Benson*	16
— *sublesta*. *Benson*	17
— subrugata. *Pfr.*	4
— *subrugata*. *Pfr.* 4,	5
— Sydneyensis. *Cox*	9
— *Sydneyensis*. *Cox*	9
— Taranaki. *Gray*	61
— Tasmaniæ. *Cox*	22
— tescorum. *Benson*	63
— Torresiana. *Homb et Jacq.*	61
— torulus. *Ferussac*	42
— Tuckeri. *Pfr.*	61
— turriculata. *Cox*	8
— *turriculata*. *Cox*	8
— Urvillei. *Homb et Jacq*	40
— Victoriæ. *Cox*	37
— villaris. *Pfr.*	2
— *villaris*. *Pfr.*	2
— vinitincta. *Cox*	18
— vitracea. See Additions	
— *vitrea Dermatocera*	45
— Walkeri. *Gray*	28
— *Walkeri Zonites*. *Gray*	28
— Waterhousei. *Cox*	3
— Wellingtonensis. *Cox*	29
— Wesselensis. *Cox.* See additions	
— Wilcoxi. *Cox*	9
— *Wilcoxi*. *Cox*	8
— Yorkensis. *Pfr.*	31
— *Yorkensis*. *Pfr.*	31
— Yulei. *Forbes*	57
— *Yulei*. *Forbes* 55,	58
— ziczac. *Gould*	18
— *Zonites Walkeri*. *Gray*	28
HYALINA. *Pfr.*	9

	PAGE
HYDRA. *Adams*	49
HYGROMIA. *Pfeiffer*	30
INOPERCULATA	1
LIPARUS. *Pfr.*	71
MACROCYCLIS. *Pfr.*	52
MESEMBRINUS. *Pfr.*	71
MICROCYSTIS. *Pfr.*	7
NAPÆUS. *Pfr.*	68
OMPHALOTROPIS. *Pfr.*	104
— malleata. *Pfr.*	104
— *malleata, Hydrocena*. *Pfr.*...	104
OPEAS. *Pfr.*	69
OPERCULATA	91
OPISOPHTHALMA. *Pfr.*	92
PARYPHANTA. *Pfr.*	5
PATULA. *Pfr.*	21
PLAGIOPTYCHA. *Pfr.*	47
PLANISPIRA. *Pfr.*	47
PNEUMONOPOMA. *Pfr.*	91
POMATIA. *Pfr.*	35
PUPA. *Lamarck*	78
— Australis. *Adams & Angas*	79
— Kingi. *Cox*	79
— Lincolniensis. *Cox*	80
— Margaretæ. *Cox*	80
— *Mastersi*. *Cox*	79
— Moretonensis. *Cox*	81
— Nelsoni. *Cox*	79
— Strangei. *Pfr.*	80
— *Vertigo Australis*. *Adams and Angas*	79
— *Vertigo Lincolniensis*. *Cox*.	80
PUPINA. *Vignard*	99
— bilinguis. *Pfr.*	100
— *bilinguis*. *Pfr.* 101,	102
— Coxi. *Marche*	100
— meridionalis. *Pfr.*	100
— Pfeifferi. *Dohrn*	103
— *Pfeifferi*. *Dohrn*	102
— pineticola. *Cox*	102
— planilabris. *Pfr.*	99
— pupinella *Whartoni*. *Cox*	99
— *pupinella MacGillivrayi*. *Cox*	100
— robusta. *Cox*	101
— Strangei. *Pfr.*	103
— *Strangei*. *Pfr.*	103
— Thomsoni. *Forbes*	102
— ventrosa. *Dohrn*	102
— Wilcoxi. *Cox*	101
PUPINEA. *Pfr.*	99
REALIEA. *Pfr.*	104
RHABDOTUS. *Pfr.*	72
RHYSSOTA. *Pfr.*	4
ROTULA. *Pfr.*	33
SUCCINEA. *Draparnaud*	87
— amphibia. *Draparnaud* .. 88,	91
— aperta. *Cox*	90
— arborea. *Adams & Angas*	89
— Australis. *Ferussac*	88
— *Australis*. *Pfr.*	88
— Eucalypti. *Cox*	90

INDEX.

	PAGE
Succinea. MacGillivrayi. *Cox*	90
— Menkeana. *Pfeiffer*	91
— Nortoni. *Cox*	90
— *oblonga. Deparnaud*	88
— *putris. Linnæus*	88
— *rhodostoma. Cox*	88
— scalarina. *Pfr.*	89
— *scalarina. Pfr.*	89
— strigata. *Pfr.*	88
— *strigata. Pfr.*	89, 90
— strigillata. *Adams & Angas*	89
— *Succinea*	88
Tachea. *Pfr.*	63
Temesa. *Pfr.*	81
Thersites. *Pfr.*	62
Trochomorpha. *Pfr.*	34
Truncatella. *Risso*	92
— Brazieri. *Cox*	93
— ferruginea. *Cox*	94
— marginata. *Küster*	92
— *marginata. Küster*	93
— Pfeifferi. *Martens*	94
— scalarina. *Cox*	93
— *scalaria*	93
— teres. *Pfr.*	92
— Yorkensis. *Cox*	93
Vallonia. *Pfr.*	61
Vertigo. *Müller*	78

	PAGE
Videna. *Pfeiffer*	31
Vitrina. *Draparnaud*	82
— Aquila. See additions	
— Australis. *Pfr.*	87
— *Australis. Pfr.*	87
— castanea. *Pfr.*	84
— Freycineti. *Ferussac*	83
— *Helix Bughyi*	83
— hyalina. *Pfr.*	85
— inflata. *Reeve*	86
— leucospira. *Pfr.*	83
— MacGillivrayi. *Cox*	86
— Mastersi. *Cox*	86
— megastoma. *Cox*	87
— Milligani. *Pfr.*	82
— nigra. *Quoy et Gaimard*	84
— *planilabris. Cox*	86
— robusta. *Gould*	84
— *section Peltella*	87
— Strangei. *Pfr.*	85
— *Strangei. Pfr.*	83, 84, 86
— *Tasmania*	84
— Verreauxi. *Pfr.*	83
— *Verreauxi. Pfr.*	84
— virens. *Pfr.*	85
— *vitrina*	85, 86
Xerophila. *Pfr.*	31
Xesta. *Pfr.*	2

AUSTRALIAN LAND SHELLS.

SUB-KINGDOM II.—MOLLUSCA.
CLASS II.—GASTEROPODA.
ORDER II.—PULMONIFERA.
SECTION A.—INOPERCULATA. SECTION B.—OPERCULATA.

SECTION A.—INOPERCULATA.
FAMILY.—HELICIDÆ.

SHELL external, usually well developed and capable of containing the entire animal; aperture closed by an epiphragm during hybernation.

Animal hermaphrodite, having a short well developed retractile head, with four cylindrical, retractile tentacles, the upper pair longest, and bearing eye-specks at their summits, the lower occasionally wanting (*Section Vertigo*). Body spiral, distinct from the foot; respiratory orifice near the base of the right ocular tentacle, small and valve-like; mouth armed with a horny, dentated, crescent-shaped upper mandible; lingual membrane oblong, central teeth inconspicuous, laterals numerous, similar.

GENUS
HELIX.—LINNÆUS.

Shell umbilicated, perforate, or imperforate, discoidal, globosely-depressed or conoidal; aperture transverse, oblique, lunar or roundish; peristome patulous or reflected, margins distinct, remote, or united by callus.

Animal with a long foot, pointed behind; lingual teeth usually in straight rows, edge teeth dentated.

I.—SECTION XESTA. *Pfr.* Vers. p. 120.

* H. villaris.   * H. circumcincta.   * H. rustica.
* H. Waterhousei.   * H. microcosmos.

1. Helix villaris. *Pfr.* Plate X. Fig. 8, *natural size and magnified.* M.C.

Pfr., Pro. Zool. Soc., 1854, p. 146.
Reeve, Conc. Icon. sp. 1375.
Helix Kreffti. *Cox, Catalogue of Australian Land Shells,* 1864, p. 21.
Shell perforated, orbicular, depressed, thin, pellucid, smooth, with microscopic striæ, very glossy, reddish-yellow; spire broadly convex; whorls 5, slightly convex, suture slightly margined, last rounded at the periphery, less convex at the base; under surface flesh coloured and opaque about the very minute umbilicus; aperture diagonal, lunate, slightly pearly within; peristome simple, thin, straight, the columellar margin rather sloping, thickened above, with a callus inwardly, and very slightly reflected outwardly.

Diameter, greatest 0·50; *least* 0·50; *height* 0·25 *of an inch.*
Habitat. Cape York.—*Cox.* Rocky Isles, near Cape Flattery.—*MacGillivray.*

I cannot venture to keep the shell formerly named by me *H. Kreffti* distinct from *H. villaris* of Pfeiffer, whose description is quite satisfactory; while that of Reeve is less so. A remarkably polished, shining, oily-looking shell of a rich honey colour, with the columella white and callous within.

2. Helix rustica. *Pfr.* Plate IX. Fig. 3 *natural size,* 3 a. *magnified.* M.C.

Pfr., in Zeit-schrift für. Malac., 1852, p. 112.
Helix inconspicua. *Forbes, Voy. Rattlesnake,* Vol. II., p. 379. Plate II. Fig. 3.
Helix impexa. *Reeve, Conc. Icon.* sp. 795.
Helix Crotali. *Cox, Catalogue of Australian Land Shells,* 1864, p. 18.
Shell minutely perforated, depressly-convex, thin, smooth, rather glossy, very faintly striated, pale horny; spire very short, obtusely conical, suture shallow, slightly margined; whorls 5, regularly increasing, rather flattened, last convex, slightly flattened above, not continued in front; aperture diagonal, lunate; peristome simple, acute, regular, columellar margin slightly expanded, and reflected above.

Diameter, greatest 0·30; *least* 0·27; *height* 0·15 *of an inch.*
Habitat. "Low Islands" in Trinity Bay, and Howick Isle, No. I.—*MacGillivray.* Flinders Range, South Australia.—*Angas.* Rapid Bay, South Australia.—*Masters.*

I have taken the description from five specimens presented to the Australian Museum by the original collector, and from the precise locality whence Forbe's specimens were derived. They are much duller than specimens from other places, which those in the Cumingian collection, described by Pfeiffer and Reeve, undoubtedly were, as they are usually more glossy, and varying in colour—being white and crystalline, pale, yellowish horny, or of a reddish tint. The

South Australian specimens from Flinder's Range, determined by Angas to be of this species, present certain differences, being of a duller aspect, more coarsely marked, and depressed. My specimens from Rapid Bay are normal.

3. Helix circumcincta. *Cox.* Plate V. Fig. 6 a. *natural size*, 6 b. *magnified.* M.C.

Helix marmorata. *Cox, Catalogue of Australian Land Shells,* 1864, p. 20.
Shell minutely perforated, depressly and roundly-convex, thin, very smooth and shining, with microscopic spiral and transverse lines along the suture and centre of last whorl, reddish-horny, pale about the umbilicus; spire widely and flatly conical, very obtuse; suture obscurely margined; whorls 5, gradually increasing, the last rounded; aperture diagonal, broadly lunate; peristome simple, thin, the columellar margin very slightly reflected above, and sometimes partially concealing the umbilicus.

Diameter, greatest 0·40; *least* 0·35; *height* 0·15 *of an inch.*
Habitat. Kiama.—*Masters.* Along the shaded banks of the Nepean River, New South Wales.—*Cox.*

As my former name *marmorata*, applicable to the animal, was found to have been in previous use, it is necessary to change it. Closely allied to the preceding, of which it would seem to be the southern representative. In one or two of my specimens there is even shown a tendency to opacity round the umbilicus, and to the white callosity of the upper part of the columella. The pale band seems to be constant. Specimens of this shell sent to Cuming for comparison were returned with the name *H. misella*, Fer.—an *imperforate* species, with the last whorl *carinated*, and having an *angularly* lunate mouth.

4. Helix Waterhousei. *Cox.*

Helix sub-angulata. *Adams and Angas, Pro. Zool Soc.*, 1863, p. 521.
Shell orbicularly-conoidal, very thin, pellucid, glassy, pale straw coloured, narrowly umbilicated; whorls flat, very finely concentrically striated, last somewhat angular at the periphery; aperture very oblique, lunately oval, broader than long; lip acute, shortly reflected, scarcely covering the umbilicus.

Length ½ *line; breadth* 3 *lines.*
Habitat. South Australia, under stones and logs.—*Angas.*
A small species, somewhat resembling *H. rustica*, Pfr., but with the last whorl sub-angular at the periphery, and with a narrow umbilicus which is nearly concealed by a short reflexion of the columellar margin.

The description is entirely taken from the work quoted above. The specific name given by Adams and Angas had, however, been applied in 1854, by Pfeiffer, to a Tasmanian species. A new name is therefore necessary.

5. Helix microcosmos. *Cox.* Plate VIII. Fig. 12. *natural size and magnified.* M.C.

Helix microscopica. *Cox.*
Cox, Catalogue of Australian Land Shells, 1864, p. 21.
Shell perforated, depressly-globose, thin, transparent, not shining,

irregularly and rather closely striately ribbed, some of the riblets more prominent than others, interstices very minutely striated and granulated, reddish-horny; spire obtusely convex; suture rather impressed; whorls 4, convex, slowly increasing, last convexly-rounded; base rather convex, which is more glossy, and less prominently ribbed than above, umbilicus minute; aperture oblique, somewhat squarely-lunate; peristome simple, outer lip slightly curved, lower more so, and columella nearly straight, slightly thickened and reflexed above.

Diameter, greatest 0·06; *least* 0·04; *height* 0·30 *of an inch.*

Habitat. Stroud.—*King.* Darling Point and Shark Bay, Sydney. Gore's Hill, Lane Cove, N. S. W.—*Brazier.*

The most minute of the Australian Helices known to me. It can be easily recognised by attending to the characters.

II.—SECTION RHYSSOTA. *Pfr.* VERS. p. 121.

* H. pudibunda. * H. subrugata, *Pfr.* * H. Moretonensis.

6. Helix pudibunda. *Cox.* Plate II. Fig. 11. M.C.

Shell perforated, depressly-turbinate, thin and transparent, very smooth, shewing under the lens very faint curved lines, and traces of still fainter spiral lines, shining, pinkish or flesh coloured; spire broadly conical, rather acute; whorls 6, flatly convex, last not descending in front, the periphery shewing nearly obsolete traces of a keel, below convex, glossy, generally opaquely milky-white about the umbilicus, which is minute and shallow; aperture diagonal, somewhat squarely-lunar, pearly within; peristome simple, acute, columellar margin very slightly triangularly dilated and reflected above. In old age, white and callous.

Diameter 0·65; *height* 0·55 *of an inch.*

Habitat. Richmond River.—*MacGillivray.* Moreton Bay.—*Masters.*

The smoothness, want of carina, pinkish colour, and callous columella are the chief points of distinction between this and *H. Moretonensis* and *H. subrugata.*

7. Helix subrugata. *Pfr.* Plate IX. Fig. 2 *natural size,* 2 a., 2 b. *magnified.* M.C.

Pfr., Pro. Zool. Soc., 1851, p. 259.
Helix Clarencensis. *Cox, Pro. Zool. Soc.*, 1864, p. 594.

Shell slightly perforated, depressly-turbinate, very thin, smooth, transparent, shining, white, olivaceous, or yellowish-horny, finely and irregularly arcuately striated, and under the microscope closely spirally striated; spire shortly conical, rather acute; whorls 6, very flatly convex, last very slightly descending in front, very obtusely carinated; base rather convex, shining, with radiating faint lines; aperture diagonal, very slightly angularly rounded; peristome simple, acute, externally bluntly angular, columellar margin above shortly triangularly dilated, scarcely reflected.

Diameter, greatest 0·42; *least* 0·40; *height* 0·25 *of an inch.*

Habitat. Clarence River, &c.—*MacGillivray.*

After comparing a large number of specimens, I have satisfied myself that this is the shell described by Pfeiffer as *H. subrugata*, although his description is too brief to ensure absolute certainty.

8. Helix Moretonensis. *Pfr.* Plate X. Fig. 2, 2 a.   M.C.
Pfr., Pro. Zool. Soc., 1851, p. 52.
Reeve, Conc. Icon. sp. 1313.
Shell perforated, conoidly-lenticular, very thin, sub-arcuately-plicate, dull above, shining below, olivaceous or yellowish-horny; spire broadly conoid, somewhat acuminate; suture simple, impressed; whorls 6, very slightly convex, last not descending in front, flattened above, convex below, rather sharply keeled; aperture diagonal, somewhat angularly lunate, pearly within; peristome acute, thin, more or less distinctly angular in front at the columella, shortly and triangularly dilated, reflected and half concealing the minute umbilicus.
Diameter, greatest 0·50; *least* 0·45; *height* 0·20 *of an inch.*
Habitat. Richmond River.—*MacGillivray.* Moreton Bay.—*Masters.*
A coarser, duller, and more angular shell than the two preceding species.

III.—SECTION PARYPHANTA. *Pfr.* Vers. p. 122.

* H. atramentaria.

9. Helix atramentaria. *Shuttleworth.* Plate III. Fig. 2 a., 2 b.   M.C.
Nanina atramentaria. *Shuttl., in Mittheilungen der Naturf. Gesellsch. in Bern.*, 1852, p. 194.
Shell umbilicated, depressed, sub-discoid, covered with a very dark blackish-purple glossy epidermis, showing numerous lines of growth, most distinct about the suture, and under the lens minute rugæ crossing them and occupying the whole upper surface; spire short, obtuse; whorls 4, convex, very rapidly increasing, last scarcely deflexed in front, depressed, and inflated; below very glossy, umbilicus 1-5th of the smaller diameter; aperture rather more than diagonally oblique, lunately-oval; peristome simple, the epidermis covering it, the right margin produced in a flexuous manner at the centre, columella very shortly expanded above and reflected, to conceal about ½ of the umbilicus.
Diameter, greatest 1·40; *least* 1·10; *height* 0·55 *of an inch.*
Habitat. Mount Arnold and Bendigo, Victoria.—*Cox.*
This very remarkable shell, like the New Zealand *Helix Busbyi* in miniature, resembles no other known Australian species.

IV.—SECTION HELICOPHANTA. *Pfr.* Vers. p. 122.

* H. Falconari.   * H. Maconelli.   * H. Banneri.

10. Helix Falconari. *Reeve.* Plate VI. Fig. 6.   M.C.
Gray, *Pro. Zool. Soc.*, 1834, p. 63.
Reeve, Conc. Icon. sp. 355.
Shell umbilicated, ovate, thin, smooth, covered with a rather glossy brownish, reddish, or yellowish epidermis, faintly rugosely striated,

crossed with fainter very minute corrugations, variously marked with interrupted dark bands and series of blotches, frequently obsolete or wanting, and usually near the suture darker and flame-like; spire small, obtuse; whorls 4, convex, very rapidly increasing, the last very much dilated and produced in front, diagonally from the axis, much compressed about the large deep and funnel-shaped umbilicus; aperture oblique, lunately oblong, bluish and somewhat iridescent; peristome thin, margins slightly approximating and joined by a very thin callus, outer nearly straight, anterior regularly curved, columellar sinuated in the centre, much expanded, and reflected in an arched manner over the umbilicus.

Diameter, greatest 3·50; least 2·60; height 2·00 of an inch.
Habitat. Manning, Bellinger, Clarence, Richmond and Tweed Rivers, N. S. W.—*MacGillivray*. Ipswich, Queensland.—*Masters*.

A variety of a uniform fulvous colour is frequently met with.

This fine species is very variable in its markings, but yet not admissible of division into varieties, with the exception of that mentioned, of which I have many specimens from the Richmond River.

11. Helix Maconelli. *Reeve.* Plate III. Fig. 5.   M.C.
Bulimus Maconelli. *Reeve, Pro. Zool. Soc.*, 1851, p. 198. *Moll.* Pl. XII.

Shell imperforate, ovate, thin, finely striated, the striæ decussated by very faint corrugated wavy lines, covered with a reddish chestnut epidermis, with numerous (4 to 8), spiral, interrupted dark bands of various width, consisting of separate rectangular blotches, with series of larger and darker markings near the suture, with yellow or paler interstices; spire short, obtuse; whorls 4, moderately convex, very rapidly increasing, last inflated and produced in front in the direction of the axis; aperture oblique, lunately oval, bluish-grey, and pearly within; peristome simple, acute, margins joined by a very thin callus, right rather straightly curved, basal regularly arcuated, columellar nearly straight, whitely callous, flatly reflected and adnate.

Diameter, greatest 3·20; least 2·20; height 2·10 of an inch.
Habitat. Brisbane, Queensland.—*Maconell*.

This has generally been regarded as a Bulimus; it is, however, so remarkably allied to *Helix Falconari*, that it seems more natural that they should be generically associated. The markings and even the minute sculpturing may be said to be identical, but the present species is more lengthened or Bulimoid, and is imperforate.

12. Helix Banneri. *MacGillivray.* M.S.S.
Pfr., *Pro. Zool. Soc.*, 1862, p. 270.

Shell umbilicated, turbinately-globose, rather thin, obliquely irregularly striated and very thickly pustulated, reddish-yellow, with a yellowish band near the suture; spire shortly turbinate, apex rather acute; whorls $4\frac{1}{2}$, convex, the last ventricose, deeply descending in front; columella slightly arched, sinuous; aperture almost diagonal, lunately rounded, somewhat pearly within; peristome thin, shortly expanded, scarcely reflected, margins converging, joined by a thin

callus, columellar extremely dilated, reflexed in a vaulted manner, adherent, and more or less completely shutting up the umbilicus.
Diameter, greatest 1·61; *least* 1·30; *height* 1·22 *of an inch.*
Habitat. Cape Direction.—*Banner* and *MacGillivray*.
The above description has been wholly taken from Pfeiffer, as I have no specimen to refer to; the original, probably still unique, is part of the Cumingian collection in the British Museum.

V.—SECTION MICROCYSTIS. *Pfr.* VERS. p. 122.

* H. Jacksoniensis. * H. radians.

13. Helix Jacksoniensis. *Gray.* Plate XI. Fig. 6, *copied from Reeve.*
Gray, Pro. Zool. Soc., 1834, p. 65.
Reeve, Conc. Icon. sp. 1462.
Shell imperforate (scarcely minutely umbilicated, *Reeve*), depressed, solid (horny, *Reeve*), slightly arcuately striated, reddish-yellow, radiated with a deeper colour; spire slightly elevated, obtuse, suture margined; whorls 5, scarcely convex, slowly increasing, last not descending, flattened at the base, and impressed in the centre; aperture scarcely oblique, lunate; peristome straight, somewhat callous within, margins distant, columella slanting.
Diameter, greatest 0·29; *least* 0·27; *height* 0·13 *of an inch.*
Habitat. Near Port Jackson.—*Cunningham?*
Never having seen this shell, of which I cannot help suspecting that the locality assigned is wrong, I have given Pfeiffer's description of it from the British Museum specimen, and apparently also that figured by Reeve, who remarks:—"An obtusely depressed, shining, horny species, streaked and tinted with burnt red." In Gray's original account, it is stated to resemble *H. nitida* in form, but to be imperforate. His measurements are—*axis* 3 *lines*; *diameter* 3½ *lines.*

14. Helix radians. *Pfr.* Plate XVII. Fig. 2, *copied from Reeve.*
Pfr., Pro Zool. Soc., 1851.
Reeve, Conc. Icon. sp. 618.
Shell imperforate, depressed, thin, smooth, very shining, horny, irregularly radiated with white streaks, spire very short, convex, suture impressed, slightly margined; whorls 4½, slightly flattened, last not descending, angular above, convex at the base, slightly impressed at the middle; aperture sub-vertical, angularly lunate; peristome extremely simple, straight, acute.
Diameter, greatest 0·35; *least* 0·31; *height* 0·16 *of an inch.*
Habitat. Port Jackson, Sydney.—*Strange.*
Description taken from Pfeiffer. Reeve remarks of it—"An extremely transparent bright horny species of simple character." He does not allude to the white radiating streaks. Its claim to be Australian I take from Pfeiffer's *Mon. Hel. Viv.*, Vol. IV., p. 17.

VI.—SECTION CONULUS. *Pfr.* VERS. p. 123.

* H. turriculata.
* H. Wilcoxi.
* H. Penolensis.
* H. Parramattensis.

15. Helix turriculata. *Cox.* Plate VIII. Fig. 11, *natural size and magnified.* M.C.

Shell minutely umbilicated, semi-globosely conical, very thin, transparent, pale horny, and somewhat glassy, very lightly striated throughout; spire conical, obtuse; whorls 6, slowly increasing, slightly convex, last keeled, not descending; base slightly sloping, very finely striated as above, and more glossy; aperture moderately oblique, angularly lunate; peristome simple, thin, slightly angular in front, columella moderately dilated above and expanded.

Diameter, greatest 0·15; *least* 0·13; *height* 0·10 *of an inch.*
Habitat. Miriam Vale, Port Curtis, Queensland.—*Blomfield.*

A delicate glassy-horny conical species, the very regular spire of which is three times the height of the base; it is nearly allied to the less trochiform, hyaline, and more coarsely sculptured species, *H. Wilcoxi.*

16. Helix Parramattensis. *Cox.* Plate VI. Fig. 10, *natural size and magnified.* M.C.

Cox, *Catalogue of Australian Land Shells*, 1864, p. 20.

Shell not umbilicated, turbinately globose, thin, shining, pale, yellowish-horny, smooth; spire obtusely conical; whorls 6, very regularly increasing, moderately convex, last more so; base convex, very glossy; aperture slightly oblique, lunate; peristome thin, simple, regular, columellar margin scarcely expanded above.

Diameter, greatest 0·19; *least* 0·16; *height* 0·14 *of an inch.*
Habitat. Parramatta.—*King.* Lyndhurst, near Sydney.—*MacGillivray.* Wollongong.—*Masters.* Botanic Gardens, Sydney.—*Brazier.*

An inconspicuous little horny conical shell, globose below, without any markings.

17. Helix Penolensis. *Cox.* Plate XI. Fig. 12, *natural size and magnified.* M.C.

Cox, *Pro. Zool. Soc.*, 1867.

Shell umbilicated, somewhat globosely-depressed, thin, very finely striately ribbed, pale fleshy-horny, slightly shining; spire broadly conical, obtuse; whorls 5, slightly convex, the last obtusely carinated, not descending in front, above rather flattened near the mouth, below more convex; aperture angularly-broadly-lunato; peristome simple, thin, right margin very slightly curved, angular at the keel, then arcuately curved, forming almost half a circle to the slightly dilated and reflected callous columella, partially concealing the small umbilicus.

Diameter, greatest 0·15; *least* 0·13; *height* 0·08 *of an inch.*
Habitat. Penola, South Australia.—*Woods.*

A rather dull, small, horny, broadly semi-conical species, allied to *H. turriculata.*

18. Helix Wilcoxi. *Cox.* Plate IV. Fig. 12, *natural size and magnified.* M.C.
Cox, *Pro. Zool. Soc.*, 1864, p. 594.

Shell minutely umbilicated, globosely-conical, very thin, shining, hyaline, glassy-white or very pale yellow, finely, regularly, and closely striated across the whorls; spire conical, obtuse, suture finely margined; whorls 6, slightly convex, the last obscurely keeled below, equalling the rest in height; aperture slightly oblique, lunate; peristome simple, thin, straight, columellar margin very briefly expanded at the base, and half covering the umbilicus.
Diameter, greatest 0·18; *least* 0·16; *height* 0·20 *of an inch.*
Habitat. Clarence and Richmond Rivers, on leaves of trees.—*MacGillivray.*

VII.—SECTION HYALINA. *Pfr.* Vers. p. 124.

* H. Sydneyensis.
* H. nitida.
* H. splendidula.
* H. ductilis.
* H. albumenoidea.
* H. minima.
* H. Lyndhurstensis.
* H. subangulata. *Pfr.*
* H. fricata.

19. Helix Sydneyensis. *Cox.* Plate IX. Fig. 16 *slightly magnified*; and Plate XVIII. Fig. 3 *natural size*, 3 a. *magnified.* M.C.
Cox, *Catalogue of Australian Land Shells*, 1864, p. 37.

Shell umbilicated, depressed, rather solid, shining, transparent, faintly and closely striated with lines of growth, yellowish-horny above; spire slightly elevated, roundly obtuse, suture very obsoletely margined; whorls 5½ to 6, slightly convex, the last not descending in front, convex, slightly depressed above; base flatly convex, opaquely whitish, umbilicus very large, equalling one-fifth of the diameter of the circumference; aperture diagonally oblique, somewhat roundly and obliquely lunate; peristome smooth, straight, margins converging, columellar not dilated or expanded.
Diameter, greatest 0·53; *least* 0·45; *height* 0·25 *of an inch.*
Habitat. Abundant in gardens and cellars about Sydney.—*Cox.*

In the above there is frequently present a spiral reddish thread below the suture. Careful comparison with specimens of the European *H. cellaria* shew in that species greater flatness of spire and of the shell generally, and there is a decided difference in the shade of colour. *H. Sydneyensis* is very closely allied to *H. glaberrima* from the Solomon Islands, in the description of which by Pfeiffer and Reeve no mention is made of the obsoletely striated markings.

20. Helix nitida. *Müller.* Plate IX. Fig. 15, 15 a. *natural size and magnified.* M.C.
Müller, *Hist. Nat. Verm.*, Vol. II., p. 32.

Shell umbilicated, depressly-globular, thin, shining, transparent, very faintly transversely striated, horny, tawny throughout; spire slightly elevated, obtusely rounded; whorls 5, moderately convex,

last rounded; base excavated about the umbilicus, which is pervious, moderate, equalling about one-seventh of the diameter.
Diameter, greatest 0·20; *least* 0·17; *height* 0·10 *of an inch.*
Habitat. Darling Point, Lyndhurst, and elsewhere about Sydney.—*Cox.*

A small flattish horny species, hollowed out about the umbilicus. Widely distributed in the localities mentioned above. It may possibly be an introduction of the European species, from which it differs in no respect.

21. Helix splendidula. *Pfr.* Plate III. Fig. 3, *natural size and enlarged.* M.C.
Pfr., Pro. Zool. Soc., 1845, p. 128.
Reeve, Conc. Icon. sp. 973.

Shell umbilicated, very much depressed, thin, transparent, shining, horny, finely and closely striated, transversely, and with very minute spiral decussating lines, of a rich tawny colour; spire very slightly projecting, very obtuse; whorls 4, rapidly increasing, slightly convex, last not produced in front where it is rather depressed above, and wide; umbilicus large, perspective, equalling ⅓ of the diameter; aperture diagonal, ovately-lunar; peristome simple, acute, above slightly curved, thin, regularly arcuate to the base of the columella, which is not dilated.
Diameter, greatest 0·35; *least* 0·30; *height* 0·10 *of an inch.*
Habitat. Moreton Bay.—*King.* Falls of the Clyde, Clarence River. —*MacGillivray.* Cape York.—*Cuming.*

A species which has a wide range along the east coast of Australia, and varies considerably in size, degree of flatness, distinctness of the striæ, colour, and glossiness. The finest specimens which I have seen are from the brushes of the Clarence and Richmond Rivers, and the same holds good with *H. Strangei*, an allied shell often found in its company.

22. Helix ductilis. *Pfr.*
Pfr., Pro. Zool. Soc., 1856, p. 385.

Shell umbilicated, discoid, thin, under the lens very closely finely striated, whitish-glassy-green; spire flat; whorls 5, flattish, gradually increasing, last not descending, depressed, rounded at the periphery, scarcely more convex at the base; umbilicus perspective, exceeding ¼ of the diameter; aperture oblique, widely lunate; peristome simple, straight, margins scarcely converging, columellar short, vertical, sub-angular at its junction with the basal.
Diameter, greatest 0·25; *least* 0·22; *height* 0·08 *of an inch.*
Habitat. Drayton Range, Queensland.—*Stutchbury.*

23. Helix minima. *Cox.* Plate XII. Fig. 8, *natural size and magnified.* Australian Museum.

Shell broadly umbilicated, discoid, shining, yellowish-horny, very finely striated above, smooth at the base; whorls 5, regularly increasing, convex, narrow, last whorl a little descending in front, suture strongly impressed; spire flat; excavated round the umbilicus; mouth lunately-rounded, lip simple, thin, not reflected at the columella.

Diameter, greatest 0·07; *least* 0·06; *height* 0·03 *of an inch.*
Habitat. Mount Wellington, Tasmania.—*Masters.*

24. Helix albumenoidea. *Cox.* Plate XII. Fig. 2, *natural size and magnified.* Australian Museum.

Shell umbilicated, flattened, thin, opalescent, opaque, bluish-white, resembling coagulated albumen, smooth, dull, not shining; spire scarcely elevated; suture impressed, margined; whorls 4½ to 5, smoothly rounded, last not descending in front, the last two whorls of a uniform diameter; base convex, of a uniform colour and aspect, with upper surface; umbilicus deep, narrow, slightly excavated round about; aperture diagonal, ovately rounded; peristome simple, blunt, margins slightly converging, columella dilated at its insertion.

Diameter, greatest 0·20; *least* 0·16; *height* 0·10 *of an inch.*
Habitat. Flinder's Range, South Australia.—*Masters.*

25. Helix fricata. *Gould.*
Nanina fricata. *Gould, Expedition Shells,* 1851, p. 32.
Reeve, *Conc. Icon.* sp. 1033.

Shell rotate, thin, greenish-horny, above slightly convex, sculptured above with frequent radiating threads, sometimes forked, beneath very smooth; umbilicus wide, deep, funnel-shaped; whorls 4½; suture impressed; aperture rounded; lip simple.

Diameter 7-10th; *axis* ½ *of a line.*
Habitat. Illawarra, New South Wales.—*Drayton.*

The above is entirely taken from Gould's original description, as quoted by Pfeiffer, in *Mon. Hel. Viv.,* Vol. III., p. 93. I doubt whether Reeve's figure is intended for the shell of Gould, as the former speaks of "the two characteristic red lines," not at all alluded to by the other.

26. Helix Lyndhurstensis. *Cox.* Plate XVII. Fig. 1 *natural size,* 1 a., 1 b. *much magnified.* Museum, R. L. King.

Shell largely and openly umbilicated, pellucid, rotundately depressed, obsoletely striated, smooth, shining; spire obtusely convex, brownish; whorls 4 to 5, the last dilated; aperture lunately-circular; peristome simple, acute.

Diameter 0·25; *height* 0·09 *of an inch.*
Habitat. Lyndhurst, Sydney.—*King.*

The only specimens which I have seen of this species are in the cabinet of the Rev. R. L. King, of Parramatta, by whose kindness I have been enabled to figure this and many other species.

27. Helix subangulata. *Pfr.* Plate IX. Fig. 6, *copied from Reeve.*
Pfr., Pro. Zool. Soc., 1854, p. 53.
Reeve, Conc. Icon. sp. 1301.

Shell umbilicated, convexly-depressed, rather solid, finely striated, scarcely shining, waxy, ornamented with a narrow chestnut band near the suture, and 2 broader ones (3 *in Reeve's Fig.*) beneath the periphery; spire short, convex, obtuse; whorls $4\frac{1}{2}$, slightly convex, gradually increasing, last not descending, periphery slightly angled, base rather flat, aperture oblique, of a rounded squarish form; peristome simple, straight, with margins nearly parallel, the columellar being expanded near the umbilicus, which is of a moderate size and open.

Diameter, greatest 0·64; *least* 0·50; *height* 0·45 *of an inch.*
Habitat. Van Diemen's Land.—*Pfeiffer.*

As I have never seen this species, I have taken the above description from Pfeiffer, *Mon. Hel. Viv.*, Vol. IV., and the figure from Reeve, *Conc. Icon.*

VIII.—SECTION DISCUS. *Pfr.* Vers. p. 125.

* H. sericatula.	* H. inusta.	* H. cochlidium.
* H. pexa.	* H. Murrayana.	* H. Brazieri.
* H. Saturni.	* H. lirata.	* H. Adelaidæ.
* H. albanensis.	* H. funerea.	* H. sublesta.
* H. Cygnea.	* H. iuloidea.	* H. Belli.
* H. vinitincta.	* H. omicron.	* H. ziczac.
* H. corticicola.	* H. mucosa.	* H. rapida.
* H. bombycina.	* H. Srondensis.	* H. Diemenensis.
* H. retepora.	* H. Morti.	* H. Tasmanica.
* H. Hobarti.	* H. cuprea.	* H. Melbournensis.
* H. Le Grandi.	* H. similia.	* H. Murphyi.

28. Helix sericatula. *Pfr.* Plate XII. Fig. 6 *natural size, and* 6 a. *magnified.* M.C.
Pfr., Pro. Zool. Soc., 1849, p. 127.
Reeve, Conc. Icon. sp. 812.

Shell perforated, depressed, discoid, thin, closely and rather finely striately ribbed, greyish-horny, rayed with dark brown, the streaks generally in clusters, not shining, but sometimes with a silky lustre; spire flat; whorls $4\frac{1}{2}$, slightly convex, last not descending in front, rounded, somewhat impressed near the umbilicus; aperture slightly oblique, lunate, sometimes pearly within; peristome simple, rather obtuse, straight, the columellar margin sloping, slightly reflected above, and partially concealing the small umbilicus.

Diameter, greatest 0·20; *least* 0·17; *height* 0·10 *of an inch.*
Habitat. Garden, Clark, and Shark Islands, in Port Jackson; also abundant in the neighbourhood of Sydney, and in other parts of the colony.—*Cox.*

A shell easily recognised, although it varies much in markings, and is sometimes without any, and entirely of a light brown. Usually the ribs are black at intervals, or wholly, giving the shell a streaked appearance.

29. Helix inusta. *Cox.* Plate X. Fig. 3, *natural size and magnified.* M.C.
Helix nautiloides. *Cox.*
Cox, Pro. Zool. Soc., 1865, p. 696.

Shell perforated, orbicularly depressed, discoid, regularly finely ribbed in an arcuately curved manner, covered with a reddish-horny epidermis, not shining; spire flat, suture impressed; whorls 4, convex, the last rounded and rather tumid, above towards the suture convex, slightly flattened towards the mouth, not descending; aperture nearly diagonal, obliquely ovately-lunate, pearly within; peristome simple, sinuated above, at first horizontal, then sloping downwards, and curved to the columella, which is slightly expanded above, and partially concealing the small umbilicus.

Diameter, greatest 0·23; *least* 0·19; *height* 0·12 *of an inch.*
Habitat. Clarence and Richmond Rivers.—*MacGillivray.*

A dull reddish-brown shell, closely allied to *H. sericatula*, but a smaller, more delicate, and a more finely ribbed species. A pale variety from the Clyde River has 5 whorls, and some small dark specimens from Greystane's, Parramatta, almost inosculate with the preceding species.

30. Helix cochlidium. *Cox.* Plate VIII. Fig 1, *natural size and magnified.* M.C.
Cox, Pro. Zool. Soc., 1867.

Shell umbilicated, depressed, sub-discoid, thin, translucent, glassy, not shining, with numerous prominent, thin, elevated, plicate ribs, regular, arcuately curved, the interstices under the lens very minutely granulated and linearly streaked, white; spire flat, suture moderate; whorls 4½, convex, the last narrow, rounded, rather flattened from without, not descending in front, but rather inflated below; below plicately ribbed as above, outer margin of umbilicus steep, and not gradually merging into the base; umbilicus wide, only slightly narrower at the bottom; aperture oblique, lunate, higher than broad; peristome simple, frequently when formed by one of the plicate ribs appearing as if expanded.

Diameter, greatest 0·09; *least* 0·08; *height* 0·04 *of an inch.*
Habitat. Clarence River, under logs with *H. iuloidea.*—*MacGillivray.*

Closely allied to the next species, but comparatively with it, strongly, and even coarsely sculptured. Named from the staircase like appearance of the umbilicus.

31. Helix pexa. *Cox.* Plate VIII. Fig. 2, *natural size and magnified.* M.C.

Shell umbilicated, depressed, discoid, thin, transparent, not shining, very regularly and closely arcuately costate, each costa generally

appearing like two coalescent interstices, not striate under the lens, pale yellowish-horny; spire flat, suture moderate; whorls 4, convex, the last narrow, rounded; below slightly shining, the costæ continued into the umbilicus, which is perspective, equalling ⅓ of the diameter; aperture nearly diagonal, lunate; peristome, simple, thin.
Diameter, greatest 0·08; *least* 0·07; *height* 0·04 *of an inch.*
Habitat. Greystanes, Prospect, near Parramatta, N. S. W.—*Cox.*
Easily distinguished from *H. cochlidium* by difference in colour, and the fineness of the minute ribs, which are also very much more numerous than in its white plicately-ribbed ally. The name is intended to apply to the neat combed-out appearance of the little ribs.

32. Helix Murrayana. *Pfr.*
Pfr., Pro. Zool Soc., 1863, p. 527.

Shell umbilicated, depressed, rather thin, very closely covered with thread-like folds, scarcely shining, brown; spire flat; whorls 5, rather convex, regularly increasing, last rounded, not descending; umbilicus equalling about ¼ of the diameter; aperture slightly oblique, roundly-lunate; peristome simple, straight, margins converging, columella scarcely dilated near the umbilicus.
Diameter, greatest 0·27; *least* 0·24; *height* 0·12 *of an inch.*
Habitat. Murray Cliffs, South Australia, under stones and among grass in the ledges.—*Angas.*
To Pfeiffer's description I may add that Angas speaks of it as a small, flattened, finely plicate species, with a large umbilicus.

33. Helix Brazieri. *Cox.* Plate XI. Fig. 18, *natural size and magnified.* Mr. Brazier's Cabinet.

Shell umbilicated, flatly discoid, thin, very closely and very finely ribbed, with, under the lens, extremely faint parallel lines between the ribs, and very much stronger decussating lines, ash grey, with occasional dark lines and streaks across the whorls; spire flat, suture deeply impressed; whorls 5, regularly increasing, last equally rounded above and below; base ribbed as upper surface, umbilicus ½ the width of the shell, perspective, very broadly conical and rounded at the bottom; aperture nearly vertical, broadly lunate; peristome simple, acute.
Diameter, greatest 0·13; *least* 0·10; *height* 0·05 *of an inch.*
Habitat. Cook's River, Sydney, N. S. W., under stones in dry places.—*Brazier.*
Allied to *H. saturni* and *H. lirata.* Its ash-grey colours and streaks resemble the commonest forms of *H. sericatula*, and the enormous proportional width of the umbilicus is very distinctive. The markings, although somewhat difficult to describe clearly, are characteristic.

34. Helix Saturni. *Cox.* Plate VI. Fig. 11, *natural size and magnified.* M.C.
Cox, *Catalogue of Australian Land Shells*, 1864, p. 35.

Shell umbilicated, flatly discoid, thin, not shining, finely and prominently ribbed, not very regularly, the interstices under the lens with fine parallel lines not decussated, reddish-horny; spire flat, suture deeply impressed; whorls 5, very regularly increasing, last equally rounded above and below; base marked as upper surface, the ribs running into the umbilicus, which is wide, perspective, and equalling ¼ of the diameter; aperture slightly oblique, lunate, peristome simple, acute.

Diameter, greatest 0·14; *least* 0·12; *height* 0·05 *of an inch.*

Habitat. Rusheutters' Bay, Darling Point, Craigend, &c., near Sydney, New South Wales.—*Cox.*

A shell easily distinguished from its allies by attention to the description.

35. Helix lirata. *Cox.* Plate XI. Fig. 3, *natural size and magnified.* M.C.

Cox, Catalogue of Australian Land Shells, 1864, p. 38.

Shell umbilicated, flatly discoid, thin, strongly and regularly, not confusedly, ribbed, the ribs rather distant, with, under the lens, the interstices occupied by thread-like lines, decussated under a higher power with still fainter lines, horny brownish chestnut; spire flat or very slightly submerged; whorls 3½, last very regularly rounded above and below; base with ribs and thread-like lines as above, umbilicus perspective, ⅓ the width of the shell; aperture vertical, semilunar; peristome simple, thin, regular.

Diameter, greatest 0·10; *least* 0·09; *height* 0·05 *of an inch.*

Habitat. Rushcutter Bay, near Sydney.—*MacGillivray.*

The nearest ally of this shell is *H. Saturni*, but the two need never be mistaken when brought together.

36. Helix Adelaidæ. *Pfr.*

Pfr., Pro. Zool. Soc., 1856, p. 387.

Shell umbilicated, depressed, keeled, rather thin, striated, white above with a brownish band; spire scarcely elevated, rather blunt at the apex, horny; whorls 4, slightly convex, last not descending, somewhat sharply keeled above the periphery, inflated at the base; umbilicus perspective, nearly equalling ¼ of the diameter; aperture almost diagonal, lunately-rounded, scarcely angular at the keel; peristome straight, very slightly lipped within, margins converging, columella somewhat spreading.

Diameter, greatest 0·24; *least* 0·20; *height* 0·12 *of an inch.*

Habitat. Adelaide, South Australia.—*Cuming.*

37. Helix albanensis. *Cox.* Plate IV. Fig. 2, *natural size and magnified.* M.C.

Shell umbilicated, depressly-convex, arcuately, closely and sharply ribbed, not shining, yellowish, with numerous short radiating reddish-brown bands; spire moderately conoid, obtuse, suture well marked; whorls 5, slowly increasing, rather convex, last rounded and somewhat inflated towards the mouth; umbilicus perspective,

½ of the diameter; aperture roundly-lunate, slightly oblique; peristome thin, simple, the margins converging and joined by a thin callus.
Diameter, greatest 0·20; *least* 0·18; *height* 0·10 *of an inch.*
Habitat. King George's Sound.—*Masters.*
The red markings are characteristic, but it does not very closely resemble the two next species from the same colony.

38. Helix funerea. *Cox.* Plate III. Fig. 1, *natural size and magnified.* M.C.

Shell umbilicated, depressed, nearly discoid, rather thin, rather strongly, regularly, and very closely arcuately ribbed both above and below, covered with dark blackish-grey epidermis with no lustre; spire flat, or very nearly so; whorls 4, convex, last rounded, not descending in front; umbilicus perspective; equalling ¼ of the diameter; aperture nearly diagonal, ovately-lunate, pearly within; peristome simple, thin, straight, columellar margin very slightly expanded.
Diameter, greatest 0·25; *least* 0·21; *height* 0·10 *of an inch.*
Habitat. Mudgee, New South Wales, in decayed logs.—*Cox.*
Apparently little subject to variation in colour, very beautifully representing *H. inusta*, but more coarsely sculptured, and having a large umbilicus.

39. Helix sublesta. *Benson.* Plate XI. Fig. 10, *copied from Reeve.*
Bens., Ann. and Mag., Nat. Hist., 1853, Vol. II., p. 30.
Reeve, Conc. Icon. sp. 1177.

Shell rather widely umbilicated, depressed, almost discoid, thin, very minutely striated like small ribs, above reddish-horny, below horny; spire scarcely elevated; suture impressed; whorls 4, slightly convex, the last not descending, roundish; umbilicus perspective, occupying almost ⅓ of the diameter; aperture vertical, roundly-lunate; peristome simple, straight, acute, margin approximating.
Diameter, greatest 0·14; *least* 0·10; *height* 0·05 *of an inch.*
Habitat. Freemantle, Western Australia.—*Bacon.*
Not having seen a specimen of this shell, the above description has been taken from Pfeiffer's *Mon. Hel. Viv.*, Vol. IV., p. 89. Benson states that it is "near *H. iuloidea*." Reeve, "on examination," declares it to be operculated, and to be a *Cyclostoma*; an opinion which Pfeiffer states is evidently erroneous.

40. Helix Cygnea. *Benson.* Plate XII. Fig 3, *copied from Reeve.*
Bens., Ann. and Mag., Nat. Hist., 1853, 2nd ser., Vol. XI., p. 30.
Reeve, Conc. Icon. sp. 1182.

Shell umbilicated, orbicularly depressed, sub-discoid, thin, brown horny, obliquely and somewhat membranously ribbed, extremely minute, descending striæ seen with the lens; spire scarcely elevated, flattened at the apex (*Pfr.*), convex (*Reeve*); whorls not quite 4½, convex, rather narrow, last not descending, rounded; umbilicus conical, almost equalling ⅓ of the diameter; aperture

scarcely oblique, roundly-lunate, *Pfr.*, nearly circular, *Reeve*; peristome simple, straight, margins somewhat approximating, columellar margin scarcely dilated, shortly reflected.
Diameter, greatest 0·16 ; *least* 0·15 ; *height* 0·06 *of an inch.*
Habitat. Perth, Western Australia.—*Bacon.*

Like the preceding, this description is not original, but extracted from Pfeiffer's *Mon. Hel Vir.*, Vol. IV., p. 89, and from Reeve, who states it to be a "light horny species, delicately encircled with fine ring-like riblets." Benson says it is "like *H. sublesta* and *H. iuloidea.*"

41. Helix iuloidea. *Forbes.* Plate XI. Fig 19, *natural size and magnified.* M.C.
Forbes, Voy. Rattlesnake, Vol. II., p. 379. Pl. II. F. 4.
Reeve, Conc. Icon. sp. 1464.

Shell umbilicated, depressly-orbicular, rather thin, regularly and closely finely ribbed, reddish-horny; spire flat, excavated in the centre, suture deep; whorls 4, convex, last rounded, rather tumid, not descending in front; umbilicus wide, deep and perspective, equalling ⅓ of the diameter; aperture very nearly vertical, lunate, higher than wide; peristome simple, thin, angulated near the body whorl.
Diameter, greatest 0·15 ; *least* 0·13 ; *height* 0·05 *of an inch.*
Habitat. Port Molle, North Australia.—*MacGillivray.* Clarence River, &c.—*Cox.*

Although varying in size and colour—for I have received not only very pale, but even pure white varieties from the Clarence River—also in the degree of excavation of the spire, it is a shell of very easy recognition.

42. Helix Belli. *Cox.* Plate VI. Fig. 3, *natural size and magnified.* M.C.
Cox, Catalogue of Australian Land Shells, p. 22, 1864.

Shell umbilicated, depressed, discoid, thin, transparent; regularly, very closely, and very finely marked with thread-like striæ, varying in colour from pale-horny, and reddish-yellow, to reddish-chestnut, slightly shining; spire flat, sometimes slightly concave; suture deeply impressed; whorls 5, very gradually increasing, convex, the last narrow, rounded, rather dilated below, not descending in front; below linearly marked as above, rather suddenly merging into the deep perspective umbilicus, which is nearly ⅓ the width of the shell; aperture lunate; peristome simple, thin, outer margin slightly curved.
Diameter, greatest 0·08 ; *least* 0·07 ; *height* 0·03 *of an inch.*
Habitat. Green Oakes, Darling Point, Sydney.—*Bell.*

A minute, very much depressed, finely striated, brownish shell, not resembling any other Australian species.

c

43. Helix vinitincta. *Cox.* Plate I. Fig. 6, 6 a. *natural size and magnified.* M.C.

Shell umbilicated, on both sides depressed, involute, thin, horny, closely covered with plait-like riblets, not shining, covered with a deep reddish-chestnut epidermis; spire concave, the whorls forming an upper, wide, spiral umbilicus, penetrating ⅓ of the thickness of the shell; whorls 4, quickly increasing, last narrower than high, convex along the periphery, with an obsolete ridge above compressed from behind; base flatly rounded, almost ribbed as above; umbilicus very open, exposing the whorls, shallow; aperture oval, twice the length from above downwards as from before backwards, almost vertical; peristome simple, very slightly thickened and everted, margins separated by the last whorl which bulges into the centre of the oval aperture.

Diameter, greatest 0·27; *least* 0·23; *height* 0·10 *of an inch.*

Habitat. Upper Richmond River, under logs in the brushes.—*MacGillivray.*

Closely allied in form to those specimens of *H. Omicron*, which have the spire submersed, but wanting the red markings, attaining a much larger size, and being of a deep vinous hue all over.

44. Helix Omicron. *Pfr.* Plate X. Fig. 1, *natural size and magnified.* M.C.

Pfr., Zeit-schrift für Malac, 1851, p. 128.
H. Ammonitoides. *Reeve, Conch. Icon.* sp. 1246.

Shell umbilicated, depressed, concave on both sides, thin, very closely covered with thread-like ribs or folds, not shining, horny, with numerous streaks and zigzag markings, straight, curved, and oblique; spire either deeply concave or level with the surface; whorls 4, very rapidly increasing, convex, last large, rounded, higher than broad, not descending in front; below plicately ribbed as above; umbilicus with steep margin, conical, about ⅓ of the diameter; aperture almost vertical, broadly-lunar; peristome simple, thin, margins remote, yet tending to converge, outer regularly curved, columellar margin slightly sinuated below and then slanting upwards.

Diameter, greatest 0·22; *least* 0·18; *height* 0·08 *of an inch.*

Habitat. Richmond River.—*MacGillivray.* Brisbane.—*Masters.* Port Curtis.—*Blackman.* *Var.* from Clarence River.

Although a variable species, it yet may be generally recognised at once by the red markings, which, however, vary in intensity, and are wanting in some small pale specimens.

45. Helix ziczac. *Gould.*
Gould, Pro. Bost. Soc., 1846, p. 166.
Gould, Expedition Shells, 1851, p. 41. Fig. 44.

Shell small, rounded, depressed, whitish-straw-coloured, painted with small, oblique, lightning-like, brown lines, and furrowed with acute, closely-set, reflected, hairy plates; beneath convex, perforated with a large stair-case-like umbilicus; whorls 6, convex, narrow; aperture sub-circular; sub-angulated at the base; lip simple, reflected near the umbilicus.

Width 0·30 ; *height* 0·18 *of an inch.*

Habitat. New South Wales.—*Gould.*

Probably allied to *H. Omicron*, which, however, has no pilosity. No reference to the spire is given in the preceding description, taken from the original, as copied by Pfeiffer, *Mon. Hel. Viv.*, Vol. 1, p. 116.

46. Helix corticicola. *Cox.* Plate VII. Fig. 7, 7 a. *natural size and magnified.* M.C.

Cox, *Pro. Zool. Soc.*, 1866, p. 374.

Shell rather widely umbilicated, depressly-circular, slightly shining, covered with a yellowish-red epidermis, above with pale radiating streaks, irregularly and rather thickly ribbed, below rather smooth, under the lens exhibiting obsolete spiral lines; spire depressed; whorls 5, slantingly-convex, very gradually increasing, last obtusely keeled, towards the mouth obsoletely so; aperture lunately-sub-circular; peristome thin, simple, not dilated at the columella.

Diameter, greatest 0·30 ; *least* 0·25 ; *height* 0·15 *of an inch.*

Habitat. Lismore, Richmond River, under bark in a pine scrub.—*MacGillivray.*

47. Helix mucosa. *Cox.* Plate XI. Fig. 14, *natural size and magnified.* M.C.

Shell umbilicated, depressly-orbicular, almost discoid, closely and irregularly striated in a wrinkled manner, rather solid, shining as if from oil or mucus; spire very widely conical, apex sunk; whorls 4½, very slowly increasing, slightly convex, last suddenly deflected in front, obsoletely keeled; base convex, rugosely striated as above, but more lightly; umbilicus perspective, nearly equalling ¼ of the diameter; aperture roundly-lunate; peristome simple, straight, margins somewhat approximating, columellar margin above, rather strongly expanded and reflexed.

Diameter, greatest 0·30 ; *least* 0·25 ; *height* 0·14 *of an inch.*

Habitat. Clarence River, under a log in a brush. — *MacGillivray.* A single specimen, in fine condition.

48. Helix rapida. *Pfr.* Plate III. Fig 9a., 9b. *natural size and magnified.* M.C.

Pfr., Zeit-schrift für Maluc., 1853, p. 54.

Reeve, Conc. Icon. sp. 1038.

Shell umbilicated, depressed, discoid, thin, horny, indistinctly rugosely striated, most strongly about the suture, decussated under the lens by minute, wrinkled, spiral lines, shining, profusely covered with deep reddish-chestnut wavy patches, mostly radiating, streaks, blotches, and spots; spire flat; whorls 3½, rapidly increasing, slightly convex, the last wide, slightly depressed above, rounded,

not descending in front; base moderately convex and gradually merging into the umbilicus, which is perspective, and nearly equals ½ of the diameter; very glossy below, markings mostly interrupted, or broken up, and zigzag; aperture oblique, lunately-rounded; peristome simple, acute, approximating at the margins.
Diameter, greatest 0·28; *least* 0·25; *height* 0·10 *of an inch.*
Habitat. Cape York, N. Australia.—*Edwards.*
This well marked species, discoid, shining, and curiously radiated with reddish-chestnut, was originally described as being from New Zealand, and a large variety, yellow, ornamented along the suture with a broad, jointed, chestnut band, as occurring in the Solomon Islands. My Australian specimens agree perfectly with Pfeiffer's description in his *Mon. Hel. Viv.*, Vol. III., p. 633, and also with specimens from the New Hebrides.

49. Helix bombycina. *Pfr.* Plate X. Fig. 11. M.C.
Pfr., Pro. Zool. Soc., 1854, p. 54.
Reeve, Conc. Icon. sp. 1314.
Shell umbilicated, depressed, discoid, thin, horny, closely, obliquely, and strongly striated, encircled with very numerous spiral bands and lines of various hues of yellow, red, and brown; spire flattened; whorls 4, rapidly increasing, nearly flat, last very large, depressed, scarcely descending in front; aperture lunately-oval; base smooth, yellowish, very glossy; umbilicus perspective, equalling ¼ of the diameter; peristome simple, thin, straight, margins approximating, outer dilated, columellar margin scarcely expanded above.
Diameter, greatest 0·57; *least* 0·55; *height* 0·30 *of an inch.*
Habitat. Mount Wellington, Tasmania.—*Le Grande.*

50. Helix Stroudensis. *Cox.* Plate XI. Fig. 1, *natural size and magnified.* M.C.
Cox, Catalogue of Australian Land Shells, p. 20, 1864.
Shell umbilicated, depressly-orbicular, nearly discoid, rather thin, translucent, not shining, with numerous close, fine, curved riblets, pale yellowish-horny; spire scarcely projecting, flat, suture deep; whorls 4, very gradually increasing, last roundly-convex; base marked as above, the riblets running into the umbilicus, which is small and pervious; aperture diagonal, lunate; peristome simple, thin, right lip sub-angular.
Diameter, greatest 0·12; *least* 0·10; *height* 0·03 *of an inch.*
Habitat. Stroud, Port Stephens, New South Wales.—*King.*
A very minute species, allied to *H. Saturni, H. lirata*, &c., but differing from all the somewhat similarly sculptured species in having a small umbilicus.

51. Helix Diemenensis. *Cox.* Plate VII. Fig 6, 6 a. *natural size and magnified.* M.C.
Cox, Pro. Zool. Soc., 1867.
Shell umbilicated, depressed, orbicular, discoid, thin, translucent, with very numerous prominent riblets, not shining, with many radiate

pale red bands; spire small, slightly prominent, suture moderate; whorls 4½, slowly increasing, slightly convex, last regularly roundly convex, not descending in front; umbilicus equalling ½ of the diameter; aperture obliquely-lunate; peristome simple, thin, straight.

Diameter, greatest 0·37; *least* 0·33; *height* 0·14 *of an inch*.

Habitat. Tasmania.—*Le Grande*.

The two specimens which I possess, and also the two in the collection of the Rev. R. L. King, are imperfect in the mouth, so that I can say nothing regarding the upper part of the columella.

Pfeiffer, in *Mon. Hel. Viv.*, Vol. IV., p. 94, says, the *Helix coma* of Gray is a "New Zealand species, and that it is even found in Van Diemen's Land." A reference to the description of *H. coma*, in Vol. III., p. 99 of the same work, indicates a very strong probability that my *Helix Diemenensis* is the same. This, however, is only noted now as a point to be attended to in due time.

52. Helix retepora. *Cox.* Plate VII. Fig. 8, 8 a. *natural size and magnified.* M.C

Cox, *Pro. Zool. Soc.*, 1867, p. 39.

Shell perforated, depressly-orbicular, rather solid, not shining, very closely, strongly and almost regularly ribbed in a radiate, curved manner, some of the ribs much more projecting than others, and at somewhat regular intervals, the interstices crossed by minute and close raised lines, giving under the lens the idea of network; dull reddish-brown; spire slightly prominent, flatly rounded, obtuse, suture distinct; whorls 4½, gradually increasing, slightly convex, last roundly convex; base sculptured as upper surface; aperture obliquely-lunate, enamelled within; peristome simple, thin; columella above triangularly dilated and reflected, half concealing the rather small umbilicus.

Diameter, greatest 0·19; *least* 0·18; *height* 0·07 *of an inch*.

Habitat. Flinder's Range, S. Australia.—*Masters*.

53. Helix Morti. *Cox.* Plate XI. Fig. 13, *natural size and magnified.* M.C

Cox, *Catalogue of Australian Land Shells*, p. 22, 1864.

Helix paradoxa. *Cox, Catalogue of Australian Land Shells*, p. 21, 1864.

Rather widely and deeply umbilicated, depressly-convex, irregularly transversely ribbed, the interstices being decussately-punctately striate; slightly shining, translucent, horny-brown; whorls 3 to 3½, moderately convex, the last rounded, not descending; spire slightly elevated, obtuse; aperture roundly-lunate, margins approaching; peristome simple, the columellar border slightly everted.

Diameter, greatest 0·08; *least* 0·07; *height* 0·04 *of an inch*.

Habitat. Green Oakes, Darling Point. Marrickville. Dawes Point, and elsewhere about Sydney. Chatsworth. Campbelltown. Clarence River. Clyde River. Dapto, in N. S. W.: also S. Australia, W Australia, and Tasmania.—*Cox*.

The lips are sometimes faintly joined by a callus, and the shell exhibits variation in the distinctness of its arched ribs which are sometimes obsolete.

54. Helix Tasmaniæ. *Cox.* Plate XII. Fig. 4, *natural size and magnified.* Australian Museum.

Shell widely umbilicated, depressed, each whorl regularly marked above with alternate dark-chestnut and light segments; regularly and strongly ribbed; thin, spire slightly raised; whorls 5, flattened towards the suture, the last a little descending in front, base convex; umbilicus deeply funnel-shaped; aperture roundly-dilated, lip simple, sharp, margins closely approaching, columellar margin not dilated at its base.

Diameter, greatest 0·13; *least* 0·11; *height* 0·07 *of an inch.*
Habitat. Mount Wellington, Tasmania.—*Masters.*

55. Helix Hobarti. *Cox.* Plate XII. Fig. 11, *natural size and magnified.* Australian Museum.

Shell openly and deeply umbilicated, depressed, dusky-brown, closely and regularly transversely ribbed; spire only slightly elevated principally produced by the depression of the last whorl; whorls 4½, rounded; base convex, with a funnel-shaped umbilicus; aperture almost round; peristome simple, margins closely approximating, no evertion of the columellar margin.

Diameter, greatest 0·12; *least* 0·09; *height* 0·05 *of an inch.*
Habitat. The Domain, Hobart Town, Tasmania.—*Masters.*
Closely allied to *H. Morti*, of New South Wales.

56. Helix cuprea. *Cox.* Plate XII. Fig. 9, *natural size and magnified.* Australian Museum.

Shell with a deep, rather large umbilicus, discoid; spire flat, but not impressed; of a light copper colour, with metallic lustre; whorls 4½ to 5, gradually increasing, last whorl rounded, closely and finely striated above and at the base, suture broad, last whorl slightly depressed in front; aperture rounded; lip simple, margins approximating, columellar margin at the base very slightly everted.

Diameter, greatest 0·10; *least* 0·08; *height* 0·06 *of an inch.*
Habitat. King George's Sound, W. Australia.—*Masters.*

57. Helix Melbournensis. *Cox.* Plate XII. Fig. 10, *natural size and magnified.* Australian Museum.

Shell umbilicated, depressly-globose, finely and regularly striated, converging towards the umbilicus, uniformly brown, lighter below than above; whorls 4½, rounded, gradually increasing, suture impressed, spire moderately elevated: aperture lunately-rounded; lip simple, margins converging, columellar margin broadly reflected at its base, covering the umbilicus.

Diameter, greatest 0·20; *least* 0·17; *height* 0·14 *of an inch.*
Habitat. Melbourne, Victoria.—*Masters.*

58. Helix Le Grandi. *Cox.* Plate XII. Fig. 7, *natural size and magnified.* Australian Museum.

Shell openly umbilicated, depressly-orbicular, rather irregularly, closely, and sharply striated, reddish-brown; spire flat, but not excavated in the centre; suture impressed; whorls 4½, flattened and slanting towards the suture, last tumid, not descending in front; umbilicus widely open, freely exposing the whorls; aperture round, lips simple, thin, margins closely approaching, columellar margin not reflected at the base.

Diameter, greatest 0·13; *least* 0·12; *height* 0·07 *of an inch.*
Habitat. Mount Wellington, Tasmania.—*Masters.*
Closely allied to, and resembling *H. inloidea.*

59. Helix similis. *Cox.* Plate XII. Fig. 12, *natural size and magnified.* Australian Museum.

Shell deeply and perspectively umbilicated, discoid, spire depressed, chestnut-brown, not shining, regularly and finely ribbed on the upper and under surface; whorls 4½, rounded, last whorl descending a little in front, suture deep and narrow; peristome simple, thin; aperture round, margins closely approximating, columellar margin not reflected at the base.

Diameter, greatest 0·08; *least* 0·07; *height* 0·04 *of an inch.*
Habitat. Mount Wellington, Tasmania.—*Masters.*

60. Helix Murphyi. *Cox.* M.C.
Cox, *Catalogue of Australian Land Shells,* p. 37, 1864.

Shell openly umbilicated, depressed, reddish-horny, slightly shining, closely and obliquely elevately ribbed and under the lens, decussately striated; whorls 5, rather plainly convex, the last sharply keeled, spire obtuse; aperture moderately oblique, triangularly ovate; peristome simple and sharp.

Diameter, greatest 0·18; *least* 0·16; *height* 0·09 *of an inch.*
Habitat. Wollongong, under stones.—*Masters.*

IX.—SECTION ANGASELLA. *Adams.*

* H. cyrtopleura.

61. Helix cyrtopleura. *Pfr.* Plate IX. Fig. 13, 13a., *copied from Journ. de Conchyl.*
Pfr., *Journ. de Conchyl.,* 1862, p. 227. Pl. X. Fig. 1.

Shell rather widely umbilicated, depressed, shaped like a *Planorbis*, rather solid, with very close arcuate thread-like ribs, whitish; spire flat; whorls 4 or 4½, scarcely convex, last more convex, almost rounded, not descending in front; aperture oblique, lunately-subcircular, shining within; peristome white, callous, margins converging, right shortly expanded, basal slightly reflected.

Diameter, greatest 0·70; *least* 0·57; *height* 0·25 *of an inch.*
Habitat. Plains in the neighbourhood of Lake Torrens, South Australia.—*Angas.*

The above description is merely a translation from Pfeiffer, who states that the specimens were "dead shells." Angas, *Pro. Zool. Soc.*, 1865, p. 521, speaks of "this strongly plicate, flattened, and widely umbilicated species" as being the type of this section.

X.—SECTION PATULA. *Pfr.* Vers. p. 126.

* H. ptychomphala.   * H. confusa.   * H. Leichhardti.
* H. capillacea.   * H. Strangei.   * H. bullacea.
* H. Franklandiensis.* H. Strangeoides. * H. Georgiana.
* H. Walkeri.   * H. lampra.   * H. lamproides.
* H. Wellingtonensis.* H. Namoiensis.   * H. Harriettae.
                     * H. Ramsayi.

62. Helix ptychomphala. *Pfr.* Plate VII. Fig. 1, 1 a.
Also Plate XVIII. Fig. 5. M.C.
Pfr., Pro. Zool. Soc., 1851, p. 98.
Reeve, Conc. Icon. sp. 760.

Shell umbilicated, depressly-globose, rather thin, very closely rugosely striated with a few nearly obsolete indications of decussating lines, shining, horny, yellowish or reddish, with irregular darker transverse streaks; spire small, convexly rounded; whorls $4\frac{1}{2}$, last roundly-swollen, not turned down in front; base convex, smooth at the umbilicus, which is usually chestnut, and surrounded by a yellow band, the opening plicated within, rather large, perspective, equalling about 1-6th the diameter; aperture moderately oblique, irregularly lunately-oval, higher than broad; peristome simple, thin, columellar margin rather straightly ascending, callous, moderately dilated and reflected.

Diameter, greatest 1·15; *least* 1·00; *height* 0·60 *of an inch.*
Habitat. Cape Upstart.—*MacGillivray.* Wide Bay.—*Stutchbury.* Manning River.—*Cox.*

63. Helix confusa. *Pfr.* Plate IV. Fig. 3; also Plate XVIII. Fig. 4. M.C.
Pfr., Pro. Zool. Soc., 1855, p. 112.

Umbilicated, conoidly-semi-globular, rather thin, very glossy, closely and regularly finely striated, yellowish, reddish or reddish-chestnut, with irregular radiating darker bands; spire short, obtusely-conical; whorls $4\frac{1}{4}$, slightly convex, last wide and inflated, not descending in front, rather flattened above; base convex, smoother and much more shining than the upper surface; umbilicus perspective, equalling 1-6th of the diameter, within uniform in colour, strongly striated; aperture very nearly diagonal, roundly-lunate, pearly within, margins approaching; peristome simple, thin, scarcely dilated at the columellar margin.

Diameter, greatest 1·45; *least* 1·25; *height* 0·60 *of an inch.*
Habitat. Ipswich.—*Masters.* Wide Bay.—*King.* Cape Upstart and Upper Richmond River.—*MacGillivray.*

Pfeiffer remarks that it differs from the nearly allied *H. ptychomphala*, in having the striae straight, and not undulated, in the last whorl being broader, sub-depressed, almost smooth, and the umbilicus of the same colour as the rest of the shell, instead of being chestnut, surrounded by a yellow band. A variety, of which I have numerous specimens from the Richmond River, differs in being duller above, in the greater completeness of the ribs which are scarcely fainter towards the mouth, and in the entire absence of the spiral lines occasionally met with in this fine species.

64. Helix Leichhardti. *Cox.* Plate V. Fig. 1. Australian Museum.
Cox, Catalogue of Australian Land Shells, p. 35, 1864.

Shell umbilicated, conoidly-semi-globular, rather thin, glossy, closely, not very regularly, and frequently anastomosedly striated, with no indications of spiral decussating lines, reddish-yellow, tinged with green, with some dark irregular radiating streaks; spire convex, obtuse; whorls 4½, moderately convex, last very large, inflated, deflected at the mouth, depressly-convex above, flattened at the mouth; below convex, a faint yellow ring round the umbilicus, which is perspective, and equals ¼ of diameter; aperture oblique, irregularly ovately-lunate, broader than high; peristome simple, plain, straight, right margin nearly straight, anterior and columellar margins gradually merging, arcuately curved, very slightly dilated and reflected above.

Diameter, greatest 1·40; *least* 1·20; *height* 0·50 *of an inch.*

Habitat. Australia.—*Leichhardt.*

65. Helix capillacea. *Fer.* Plate VI. Fig. 7; and Plate XI. Fig. 8. M.C.
Fer., Hist., p. 206. Pl. LXXXII. F. 5.

Shell umbilicated, depressed, closely and almost regularly striated, thin, glossy, horny-yellow; spire scarcely or not at all showing; whorls 4, quickly increasing, flatly-convex, last very large, depressly-convex, not descending in front; base more convex, smoother, more glossy; umbilicus pervious, about 1-5th of diameter; aperture diagonal, transversely, lunately-oval, wider than high; peristome simple, thin, straight, margins approximating, columellar margin very slightly expanded.

Diameter, greatest 0·95; *least* 0·80; *height* 0·27 *of an inch.*

Habitat. Garden Island, Port Jackson, &c.—*Cox.*

Specimens of a shell from Garden Island, Port Jackson, in my collection, so thoroughly agree with the description of Ferrusac of *H. capillacea,* copied in Pfeiffer's *Mon. Hel. Viv.,* Vol. I., p. 90, and as perfectly with the three figures in the original plate, with which I have carefully compared them, that I have not the slightest hesitation in referring them to that species originally stated as from Port Jackson. And as this is merely one of the forms of a very variable species, long afterwards named *H. Strangei* by Pfeiffer, the latter name should be regarded as a synonym. However, to compromise the matter, I here beg to include under the head *H.*

capillacea all those shells of the Port Jackson type, with the spire flat, or nearly so, and for the group, much depressed, and finely and closely ribbed, without any decussating spiral lines.

I possess a large specimen from the shores of Port Jackson, 1·00 *by* 0·85 *of an inch*, very rudely sculptured, and from the prominence of the lines of growth evidently an old shell, in which there are no spiral lines, and where the spire is quite flat.

66. Helix Strangei. *Pfr.* Plate XVIII. Fig. 17. M.C.

Pfr., Pro. Zool. Soc., 1848, p. 108.
Reeve, Conc. Icon. sp. 416.

Shell umbilicated, depressed, rather thin, shining, pellucid, closely striately-ribbed above, decussated with very numerous impressed spiral lines, yellowish, reddish, or chestnut-horny; spire slightly elevated, obtuse; whorls 5, slightly convex, last large, tumid, depressed above, convex externally and below, not descending in front; base nearly smooth, with obsolete indications of striæ and concentric lines, very glossy; umbilicus rather large, about 1-5th of the diameter, pervious; aperture moderately oblique, lunately-oval within, somewhat pearly; peristome simple, thin, straight, margins approximating, right rather straight, outer regularly arched, columellar margin thinly expanded, and reflected above.

Diameter, greatest 1·05; *least* 0·90; *height* 0·40 *of an inch*.

Habitat. Brisbane Water. Lane Cove. Penrith. Also Clarence, Richmond, and other rivers, as far north as Port Denison.—*Cox.*

This species is subject to considerable variation. The spiral decussating lines are sometimes absent, thus indicating a passage to *H. capillacea*; but these specimens are not so depressed, nor is the spire so flat; usually the shell looks as if varnished, and the rib-like striæ, except towards the apex, are never so prominent as in *H. capillacea*; indeed, the last are occasionally almost obsolete, as in a specimen from Ash Island, Hunter River. Examples from the brushes often exhibit, especially on the under surface, a fine deep chestnut hue, and in such situations this shell attains to its greatest dimensions. The measurements, however, are not those of one of the largest size.

67. Helix bullacea. *Pfr.* Plate IV. Fig. 11; and Plate II. Fig. 10. M.C.

Pfr., Pro. Zool. Soc., 1854, p. 53.
Reeve, Con. Icon. sp. 1288.
Helix assimilans. *Cox, Pro. Zool. Soc.*, 1864, p. 593.

Shell umbilicated, convexly-depressed, thin, glossy, pellucid, above very closely set with distinct thread-like striæ, reddish-horny; spire small, slightly convex; whorls 4, quickly increasing, rather convex, last rounded and smooth at the periphery, slightly depressed above at the mouth, rather inflated outwardly, not descending in front; base convex, very faintly radiately striated, yellowish-horny, very glossy; umbilicus moderate, 1-5th of the diameter; aperture diagonal, almost roundly-lunate, slightly iridescent within; peristome simple, thin, straight, margins convergent, sometimes joined by a very thin callus, columellar margin above triangularly dilated and reflected.

Diameter, *greatest* 0·70 ; *least* 0·55 ; *height* 0·25 *of an inch*.

Habitat. Clarence and Richmond Rivers.—*MacGillivray*.

As I have reason to suspect the shell I formerly named *H. assimilans* to be that previously described as *H. bullacea*, of Pfr., I have here placed them under one description, but with much uncertainty. My specimens agree sufficiently well with Pfeiffer's description, *Mon. Hel. Viv.*, Vol IV., p. 92; but when I compare them with Reeve's figure, to which Pfeiffer refers, I see that this does not agree, being prominently striped, with the letter press, which gives the colour as ash-horny, treats of spiral striæ, and whorls obsoletely-roundly-keeled at the periphery. Consequently, this second reference, instead of being of assistance, tends only to confound the matter, for both refer to the Cumingian cabinet for the type specimen.

68. Helix Franklandiensis. *Forbes.* Plate III. Fig. 7. M.C. *Forbes, Voy. Rattlesnake*, Vol. II., p. 372. Pl. II. F. 2, a. b.

Shell umbilicated, rather flatly-orbicularly-depressed, thin, very glossy, yellowish-horn colour, faintly striated, with numerous irregular radiating darker streaks; spire very small, nearly flat; whorls 5, slightly convex, last convex, very much dilated, slightly depressed near the mouth; base convex, of same tint as upper surface and equally shining; umbilicus wide, perspective, equalling rather more than ¼ of the diameter; aperture nearly diagonal, roundly or slightly ovately-lunate; peristome thin, simple, straight, margins approximating, columellar margin not dilated above.

Diameter, *greatest* 1·10 ; *least* 0·95 ; *height* 0·45 *of an inch*.

Habitat. Frankland and Lizard Isles, Queensland.—*MacGillivray*.

N.B.—*This species is referred by Pfeiffer to his section Discus.*

69. Helix Strangeoides. *Cox.* Plate XVII. Fig. 3, *natural size*. Fig. 3 a., 3 b. *much magnified.*
Cox, Catalogue of Australian Land Shells, p. 20, 1864.

Shell umbilicated, very depressly-orbicular, somewhat discoid, thin, transparent, shining, irregularly and rather coarsely striated, decussated with numerous fine, close, spiral lines, yellowish-horny; spire very slightly prominent, rounded; whorls 4, very rapidly increasing, last depressed above, roundly-convex outwardly and below; base smooth, with faint markings; umbilicus large, open, nearly ¼ of diameter; aperture lunately-ovate; peristome simple, thin, margins approaching.

Diameter, *greatest* 0·40 ; *least* 0·33 ; *height* 0·15 *of an inch*.

Habitat. Moreton Bay.—*King*.

Distinguished from *H. splendidula* by the possession of the spiral decussating lines. Four specimens in the collection of the Rev. R. L. King are all that I have seen.

70. Helix Georgiana. *Quoy et Gaimard.* Plate XIX. Fig. 1.
Quoy et Gaimard, Voy. de l'Astrol. et Zelée. Moll., p. 129. Pl. X.
F. 26—30.
Desh., in Fer. Hist. Moll. 1, p. 88. N. 119. Pl. LXXXIV. F. 3—4.
Shell sub-discoid, depressed, thin, brittle, translucent, yellow, above very finely and deeply striated, beneath smooth and widely umbilicated; spire very short; whorls 4, slightly convex, last large; aperture oblique, simple, sub-circular.
Diameter 0·43; *height* 0·24 *of an inch.*
Habitat. King George's Sound.—*Quoy et Gaimard.*

The above is a translation of Deshaye's description, in preference to the original one of its first describers. The figures indicate a shell of the size of *H. splendidula*, but with exceedingly delicate, regular ribbed lines throughout, even descending into the umbilicus.

71. Helix Walkeri. *Gray.*
Zonites Walkeri. *Gray, Pro. Zool. Soc.*, 1834, p. 63.
Shell depressed, umbilicated, polished, yellowish-brown; whorls 3½, very quickly increasing, ventricose, finely concentrically striated above with dense spiral striae; umbilicus deep; aperture large.
Axis 8 *lines*; *diameter* 1 *inch.*
Habitat. About seventy miles from Port Macquarie.—*Cunningham.*

This must be closely allied to *H. capillacea*, and *H. strangei*. The original description is given verbatim, as I have not seen an authentic specimen, nor has Pfeiffer. It appears to me that the word "concentrically" is a mistake for "radiately;" the fact of "spiral" or concentric striæ having been subsequently mentioned indicates this.

72. Helix lampra. *Pfr.* Plate X. Fig. 9.   M.C.
Pfr., Pro. Zool. Soc., 1854, p. 53.
Reeve, Conc. Icon. sp. 1295.
Shell umbilicated, convexly-depressed, thin, horny, translucent, very glossy, with fine arcuate rib-like striæ, from dark green to deep greenish-chestnut; spire small, convex, obtuse; whorls 4, quickly increasing, last depressed, expanded outwardly, not descending in front; base smoother, bright greenish-yellow; umbilicus about 1-5th of the diameter; aperture lunately-oval, nearly diagonal; peristome simple, thin, straight, margins converging, columellar margin very slightly reflexed above.
Diameter, greatest 0·90; *least* 0·70; *height* 0·30 *of an inch.*
Habitat. Launceston, Tasmania.—*Gunn.*

A remarkably glossy species, occasionally of a uniform olive green.

73. Helix lamproides. *Cox.* Plate X. Fig. 13.   M.C.
Cox, Pro. Zool. Soc., 1867.
Shell umbilicated, convexly-depressed, thin, closely and irregularly striately ribbed, above scarcely shining, below more so, horny-reddish, paler beneath; spire small, slightly convex, obtuse; whorls

4, quickly increasing, last not descending, depressed above, beneath convex, bluntly angular; aperture oblique, lunately-rounded; peristome simple, thin, margins converging, right straight, angular in front, columellar margin arched, neither dilated nor reflexed.
Diameter, greatest 0·57; *least* 0·50; *height* 0·22 *of an inch.*

Habitat. N.W. coast of Tasmania.—*Cox.*

Closely allied to *H. lampra*, but differing in being more coarsely sculptured, and wanting the extreme polish of that species, besides being obtusely carinated, and having the aperture angular externally.

74. Helix Wellingtonensis. *Cox.* Plate VII. Fig. 5, 5 a. *natural size and magnified*.
Cox, *Pro. Zool. Soc.*, 1867.

Shell umbilicated, depressly-orbicular, sub-discoid, thin, with thread-like riblets radiating sub-arcuately, frequently extending even to the umbilicus, not shining, varying in colour from glassy-white to dirty yellow; spire small, scarcely elevated; whorls 4, slowly increasing, moderately convex, last more convex, not descending in front; umbilicus perspective, equalling ⅓ of the diameter; aperture moderately oblique, lunate; peristome simple, thin, straight, margins approaching, columellar margin neither dilated nor reflexed.
Diameter, greatest 0·27; *least* 0·23; *height* 0·14 *of an inch.*

Habitat. Mount Wellington, Tasmania.—*Cox.*

Closely allied to *H. Diemenensis*, but differing in sculpture, in having fewer and more thread-like ribs, and also in other respects.

75. Helix Namoiensis. *Cox.* Plate XVIII. Fig. 10, 10 a. M.C.

Shell deeply, rather narrowly umbilicated, thin, transparent, shining, very smooth everywhere, light olive-brown, orbicularly depressed; spire but little raised; whorls 5, rounded, last dilated, not descending in front; aperture large, obliquely ovately-rounded, opalescent within; peristome simple, lip thin and sharp, darkened on the outer surface, margins approaching, columellar margin slightly dilated at the base.
Diameter, greatest 0·93; *least* 0·75; *height* 0·53 *of an inch.*

Habitat. Namoi River, N.S.W.—*Scott.*

This fine species presented to me by my friend, Mr. Walker Scott, much resembles *H. strangei* and other allied species in general aspect, but is at once distinguished from it by the absence of any sculpture on the upper surface, by the smallness of the umbilicus, and by the dark outer surface of the peristome.

76. Helix Harriettæ. *Cox.* Plate XVIII. Fig. 9, 9 a.

Shell largely and openly umbilicated, flatly-depressed, thin, pale, yellowish-brown, shining, coarsely striated on the upper surface, smooth at the base, irregularly streaked with dark brown and yellowish-brown; spire flattened; whorls 4, rather rapidly increasing, flat above, convex below, giving to the last whorl a blunt angled

appearance, no depression of last whorl; peristome irregularly rounded, lip simple, sharp, margins closely approximating, columellar margin moderately reflexed at the base; umbilicus equalling ½ the diameter of the shell.
Diameter, greatest 0·54; *least* 0·42; *height* 0·33 *of an inch.*
Habitat. Richmond River.—*Ramsay.*
Closely resembling young specimens of *H. Franklandiensis.*

77. Helxi Ramsayi. *Cox.* Plate XVIII. Fig. 11, 11 a.

Shell broadly and largely umbilicated, sub-discoid, depressed, covered with a thin, smooth, bright olive epidermis, rugosely striated; spire but little elevated; whorls 4½ to 5, rapidly increasing, last whorl round, broader and much dilated, very slightly deflected in front; umbilicus large and open, exposing the other whorls; aperture horizontal, large, ovately-rounded, bluish-white within, lip simple, margins approximating, not reflected at the columella.
Diameter, greatest 1·30; *least* 0·90; *height* 0·60 *of an inch.*
Habitat. Richmond River.—*Ramsay.*
This fine species may be at once recognised from all others of its type by the large inflation of the last whorl.

XI.—SECTION HYGROMIA. *Pfr.* Vers. p. 127.

* H. Jervisensis.   * H. Gilberti.

78. Helix Jervisensis. *Quoy et Gaimard.* Plate I. Fig. 2, 2 a. M.C.

Quoy et Gaimard, Voy d'Astr. II., t. 10, f. 26—30.
Reeve, Conc. Icon. sp. 758.
Shell perforate, depressly conoidly-globose, thin, fragile, obliquely striated with some irregularity, and granulated under the lens, transparent, of a pale-horny tint, generally red about the suture, and the umbilical region; spire conical, and somewhat obtuse; whorls 5, somewhat convex, the last inflated, and slightly keeled at the circumference; aperture large, oblique, rotundately-lunate; peristome with a thin rose coloured lip, and with margins apart; columella dilated above, into a somewhat broad plate, half covering the perforation.
Diameter, greatest 0·92; *least* 0·73; *height* 0·75 *of an inch.*
Habitat. Jervis Bay.—*Quoy et Gaimard.* Brisbane Water.—*MacGillivray.* Botany Bay Swamps.—*Cox.* Lane Cove, N.S.W.—*Brazier.*
This species is abundant about the swamps near Botany Bay, and agrees so thoroughly with the characters as given by Pfeiffer—*Mon. Hel. Viv.*, Vol. III., p. 118—that I have thought it better to give a translation of his original description.

79. Helix Gilberti. *Pfr.* Plate I. Fig. 8; and Plate XVIII. Fig. 7. M.C.

Pfr., Pro Zool. Soc., 1845, p. 127.
Shell umbilicated, depressed, distinctly striated, very minutely granulated, thin, of a pale-horny tint, ornamented by a red line at the

suture; whorls 4½, somewhat convex, the last convex at the base; umbilicus moderate and pervious; aperture rotundately-lunar; peristome simple and straight, with the columellar margin very little dilated and reflected.

Diameter, greatest 1·12; *least* 0·84; *height* 0·78 *of an inch.*

Habitat. Darling Downs, Queensland.—*Gilbert.* Brisbane Water.—*MacGillivray.* Hunter River, &c.—*Cox.*

The above description is taken from Pfeiffer's *Mon. Hel. Viv.*, Vol. I., p. 108, published in 1848. Subsequently, in 1859, he mentions in *Supplement* IV. of same work, that his previous description of this species was taken from an imperfect specimen. In its adult state, he states that, "it is extremely like *H. Jervisensis*; its *greatest diameter,* 22; *least* 18; *height* 13½ mill. The right margin of the peristome is somewhat expanded; the columella of a violet tint, and reflected over the umbilicus. It differs from *H. Jervisensis* in being a more solid shell, by the more gradual increase of the whorls, and by the less inflation of the last."

XII.—SECTION XEROPHILA. *Pfr.* Vers. p. 130.

* Australis.

80. Helix Australis. *Menke.* Plate IX. Fig. 7, *copied from Reeve.*
Menke, Moll. Nov. Holl., p. 6.
Reeve, Conc. Icon. sp. 803.

Shell umbilicated, orbicularly-convex, smooth, obsoletely striated, whitish, painted with obsolete grey radiating spots, and interrupted bands; whorls 5, rapidly increasing; umbilicus narrow, open; aperture wide, throat ferruginous.

Diameter, breadth 4; *height* 2—3 *lines.*

Habitat. Mount Eliza, Swan River, Western Australia.—*Priess.*

Reeve's figure represents three conspicuous spiral bands on the last whorl. The above is simply a copy of Menke's original description which Pfeiffer also copies.

XIII.—SECTION VIDENA. *Pfr.* Vers. p. 131.

* H. Launcestonensis.   * H. bisulcata.
* H. Sinclairi.   * H. Hamiltoni.
* H. Lizardensis.

81. Helix Launcestonensis. *Reeve.* Plate VII. Fig. 4, 4a. M.C.
Reeve, Pro. Zool. Soc., 1852, p. 31. Pl. XIII. F. 11.
Reeve, Conc. Icon. sp. 968.

Shell umbilicated, conoid, solid, opaque, not shining, finely granulated, and closely covered above with wrinkled and granular elevated ridges, and spiral lines of various sizes, variegated with yellowish-green and black; spire broadly-conical, rather obtuse; whorls 5, very slightly convex, slowly increasing, last acutely keeled, suddenly descending in front; base convex, very smooth, shining, deep black, with a very narrow yellow line under the periphery, sometimes wanting, and a broad bright-yellow band beneath; umbilicus rather large, perspective; aperture very oblique, lunately-elliptical; peristome somewhat simple, margins converging, right slightly curved, then a strong sinuation in front, columellar margin slightly curved, moderately thickened, and slightly reflected.

Diameter, greatest 1·30; *least* 1·20; *height* 0·65 *of an inch.*
Habitat. Tasmania.—*Gunn.*

82. Helix bisulcata. *Pfr.* Plate IX. Fig. 19, *copied from Reeve.*
Pfr., Pro. Zool. Soc., 1852, p. 135.
Reeve, Conc. Icon. sp. 969.

Shell widely umbilicated, convexly-depressed, spirally and very minutely obliquely wrinkle-striated, shining, tawny-chestnut; spire shortly conoidly-convex, slightly obtuse at the apex; suture impressed; whorls 6½, slightly convex, last much wider, periphery obsoletely angular, not descending in front, base flat, sub-compressed about the umbilicus, on both sides impressly furrowed in the middle; aperture small, slightly oblique, sub-triangularly-lunate; peristome rather simple, margins scarcely converging, right straight, sloping, basal slightly arched, somewhat thickened.

Diameter, greatest 1·14; *least* 0·98; *height* 0·50 *of an inch.*
Habitat. Tasmania.—*Gunn.*

Reeve remarks of this, that it is Solariiform, that the lip is simple, peculiarly wart-toothed within, along the line formed by the impressed groove.

83. Helix Sinclairi. *Pfr.* Plate VII. Fig. 3 a., *natural size,* 3, *slightly enlarged,* 3 b., *a portion magnified.* M.C.
Pfr., Zeit-schrift für Malac., 1845, p. 154.
Reeve, Conc. Icon. sp. 1414.

Shell umbilicated, depressed, thin, **translucent, not shining**, very regularly and very closely, rather prominently, **ribbed**, horny-yellowish, with many interrupted spiral reddish bands; spire flattened; whorls 4, flatly-convex, **quickly increasing**, last large, depressed, convex externally, much **deflected in front**; base smoother and more glossy, umbilicus widely funnel-shaped, nearly equalling ½ of the diameter; aperture diagonal, ovately-lunar; peristome simple, thin, regular, margins approximating, columellar margin scarcely dilated or reflected.

Diameter, greatest 0·70; *least* 0·60; *height* 0·25 *of an inch.*
Habitat. Mount Wellington and elsewhere, in Tasmania.—*Cox.*

As Reeve remarks, this species is chiefly remarkable for its beautiful close-set ribbed sculpture.

84. Helix Hamiltoni. *Cox.* Plate VII. Fig. 2, *natural size,* 2 a. *enlarged.* M.C.
Cox, Pro. Zool. Soc., 1867.

Shell umbilicated, sub-discoid, convexly depressed, thin, very closely and sub-arcuately ribbed, interstices with extremely fine thread-like lines, crossed by extremely minute spiral ones, giving the shell, under the lens, a linearly granular appearance, not shining, pale reddish-horny; spire small, scarcely projecting, sometimes flat, suture impressed; whorls 5, rapidly increasing, flatly-convex, last somewhat inflated, roundly convex, not descending in front, at the mouth moderately flattened above; base with the striæ smaller; umbilicus perspective, nearly equalling 1-5th of the diameter; aperture diagonal, lunately-oval; peristome simple, thin, straight, margins approaching, columellar margin above moderately dilated and reflected.

Diameter, greatest 0·70; *least* 0·50; *height* 0·20 *of an inch.*

Habitat. Mount Wellington, Macquarie Harbour, and N.E. coast of Tasmania.

A small dark variety from the last mentioned locality has the decussating striæ nearly obsolete.

85. Helix Lizardensis. *Pfr.* Plate IV. Fig. 1, *natural size and magnified.* M.C.
Pfr., Pro. Zool. Soc., 1862, p. 269.

Shell umbilicated, lenticular, carinated, slightly solid, under the lens, striately ribbed, with a conspicuous spiral raised line or rib, or second keel along, and slightly above the keel and suture, greenish-horny; spire conically-convex; whorls 8, very slowly increasing, rather flattened; base convex, somewhat coarsely ribbed under the lens, umbilicus rather large, deep, equalling 1-5th of the diameter; aperture oblique, narrowly angularly-lunate; peristome simple, straight, not dilated above.

Diameter, greatest 0·28; *least* 0·26; *height* 0·13 *of an inch.*

Habitat. Lizard Island, on the ground among dead leaves, &c.—*MacGillivray.*

Not liable to be confounded with any other Australian species of *Helix.*

XIV.—SECTION ROTULA. *Pfr.* VERS. p. 131.
* H. Indica.

86. Helix Indica. *Pfr.* Plate IX. Fig. 10, *copied from Reeve.*
Pfr., Symbolæ, Vol. III., p. 66.
Reeve, Conc. Icon. sp. 1290.

Shell umbilicated, orbicularly-convex, rather solid, rib-like striated on the upper part, and closely granulately decussated by impressed lines, fulvous; whorls 5 to 6, rather flat, the last more convex at the base, smooth, marked with a few impressed concentric lines below the keel; aperture angularly-lunar; lip straight, white, columellar margin rather thickened, shortly reflected.

Diameter, greatest 0·80; *least* 0·63; *height* 0·55 *of an inch.*

Habitat. Moreton Bay, Queensland.—*Strange.*

Never having seen specimens of this well known Indian species, I have taken the description of it from Reeve.

D

XV.—SECTION TROCHOMORPHA. *Pfr.* Vers. p. 132.

* H. Yorkensis.   * H. cumulus.   * H. Ophelia.

87. Helix Yorkensis. *Pfr.* Plate IX. Fig. 8, *copied from Reeve*. M.C.
Pfr., Pro. Zool. Soc., 1854, p. 145.
Reeve, Conch. Icon. sp. 1372.

Shell with an almost covered perforation, turbinately-depressed, thin, sculptured with hair-like striæ, silky, somewhat reddish and horny; spire convexly-conoid, apex fine, suture smooth, simple; whorls 5, slightly convex, gradually increasing, last not descending, slightly angled at the circumference; base somewhat shining, impressed in the centre; aperture diagonal, rotundately-lunar, of a somewhat pearly-reddish tint within; peristome simple, straight, margins slightly approached; columella callus, and dilated above the perforation.
Diameter, greatest 0·39; *least* 0·33; *height* 0·19 *of an inch*.
Habitat. Cape York, North Australia.—*MacGillivray*.
Specimens received from the late Mr. Cuming, labelled *H. Yorkensis* so thoroughly disagree with the above description of Pfeiffer's that I have thought it advisable not to figure them, but rather to copy Reeve's figure, with which it agrees.

88. Helix cumulus. *Pfr.* Plate IX. Fig. 11, *copied from Reeve*.
Pfr., Pro. Zool. Soc., 1854, p. 145.
Reeve, Conc. Icon. sp. 1368.

Shell perforate, turbinately semi-globose, thin, very slightly striated, shining, brown-yellow, horny: spire convexly-conoid, apex fine, slightly projecting; suture smooth, scarcely margined: whorls 5½, slightly convex, slowly increasing, the last not descending, moderately angled at the circumference, a little convex at the base; aperture diagonal, lunate; peristome simple, straight, margins separated, columellar margin a little arched, slightly dilated and reflected above.
Diameter, greatest 0·39; *least* 0·35; *height* 0·19 *of an inch*.
Habitat. Manning River, New South Wales.—*Pfeiffer*.
Not having seen this species, I have taken Pfeiffer's characters of it, and given Reeve's figure. A variety of larger dimensions is noted by Pfeiffer.

89. Helix Ophelia. *Pfr.* Plate IX. Fig. 4, *natural size and magnified*. M.C.
Pfr., Pro. Zool. Soc., 1854, p. 146.
Reeve, Conch. Icon. sp. 1345.

Shell perforate, turbinately-depressed, thin, under the lens irregularly marked with hair-like striæ, scarcely shining, diaphanous, horny, marked with narrow reddish streaks; spire convexly-conoid, apex fine, pointed; whorls 5, flattish, rather prominent, gradually increasing in size, the last not descending, moderately angled, rather flattened at the base; aperture oblique, rotundly-lunate, shining within; peristome simple, straight, margins slightly converging, basal margin somewhat narrowed; columella sloped, and near the umbilicus, which is very narrow but perforate, slightly reflected.

Diameter, greatest 0·31; *least* 0·27; *height* 0·18 *of an inch.*

Habitat. Cape York, North Australia.—*Edwards.*

The shell figured, exactly corresponds with Pfeiffer's description, as here given; but not with the figure and description of this species given by Reeve, as copied in Plate XVII. Fig. 17.

XVI.—SECTION CYSTICOPSIS. *Pfr.* Vers. p. 133.

* H. irradiata.

90. Helix irradiata. *Gould.*

Gould, *Expedition Shells*, p. 25. Pl. 5. Fig. 65.

Shell imperforate, conically globose, thin, whitish, above radiately tessellated with purple, and striated with closely set acute lines of growth, below rounded; whorls 6, convex, the last somewhat angular; aperture transverse, lunate; peristome acute, incurved towards the columella, and scarcely reflected.

Width, ¼; *height*, ⅖ *of an inch.*

Habitat. New Holland.—*Gould.*

The above description is taken from Gould. Pfeiffer states that it neither agrees with the figure, nor the dimensions.

XVII.—SECTION POMATIA. *Pfr.* Vers. p. 133.

* H. Grayi.	* H. Victoriae.	* H. Mulgoae.
* H. coriaria.	* H. expeditionis.	* H. Scotti.
* H. subgranosa.	* H. marcescens.	* H. Stutchburyi.
* H. laesa.	* H. monacha.	* H. Greenhilli.

91. Helix Grayi. *Pfr.* Plate VI. Fig. 5; Plate I. Figs. 4 and 9; and Plate X. Fig. 7. M.C.

Pfr., Symbolæ, Vol. III., p. 68.

Reeve, Con. Icon. sp. 755.

Shell with the umbilicus partially concealed, globosely-depressed, rather thin, striated and granulated all over, of a pale horny-yellow; the suture and basal area of a purple-chestnut, with the spire very little elevated; whorls 5 to 5½, somewhat convex, the last reflexed for a short distance in front, umbilicus narrow; aperture lunate, circular, lip slightly rose-coloured within; peristome simple, right margin straight, the columellar margin dilated, reflected, and rose coloured.

Diameter, greatest 1·15; *least* 1·00; *height* 0·95 *of an inch.*

Habitat. Brisbane Water. Ash Island. Hunter River. Clarence River, and other rivers as far as Brisbane, north of Sydney. Also as far south of Sydney as Ulladulla, but never far from the sea coast.—*Cox.*

As a general rule this species is easily distinguished by the purple-red band which surrounds the umbilicus, and follows the suture; but by relying on this character alone, it is apt to be confounded with

H. Gilberti and *H. Jerrisensis*; varieties of it are frequently of a dark chestnut colour, Plate I. Fig. 9, others of a pale straw colour, Plate X. Fig. 7, where the presence of the band at the suture and round the umbilicus are altogether wanting. A third variety also occurs, Plate I. Fig. 4, where the shell is surrounded with a broad pale-yellow band.

92. Helix coriaria. *Pfr.* Plate II. Fig. 7. Plate VIII. Fig. 10 ; and Plate X. Fig. 5. M.C.

Pfr., Zeit-schrift für Malac., 1847, p. 145.
Reeve, Conc. Icon. sp. 417.
Helix Mastersi. *Cox, Catalogue of Australian Land Shells*, p. 19, 1864.

Perforated, depressly-globose, solid, slightly shining, radiately striated, very finely and closely granulated, bright or dark-chestnut, paler towards the apex; spire widely conoid, obtuse at the apex; whorls 6, gradually increasing, moderately convex, last descending in front; base shining, obsoletely granulated, but the radiate striæ very distinct at the umbilicus; aperture lunately-rounded, within livid, pearly; peristome straight, obtuse, expanded, white or bluish, margins distant, columellar margin thickened and reflected, above triangularly expanded and almost entirely covering the umbilicus, leaving merely a narrow fissure.

Diameter, greatest 1·35; *least* 1·10; *height* 0·90 *of an inch*.

Habitat. Clarence River.—*MacGillivray.* Kiama. Ulladulla. Merimbula.—*Masters.* Nulla Mountains. Ash Island, N.S.W.—*Cox*.

The locality of the specimen in the Cumingian collection, described by Pfeiffer and figured by Reeve, who copies the original description, was doubtful, but in Vol. IV., p. 167, of *Mon. Hel. Viv.*, it is stated that there is a variety, of a dirty yellow colour, from Western Australia. My description is taken from specimens from Kiama and the Clarence River Heads, representing the type. But this species varies considerably, inosculating even with *H. Grayi*. A remarkable variety of great size from Kiama, chestnut below and yellowish above, with white lip, is figured in Pl. VIII., Fig. 10. A pink lip is usual among those from Merimbula, Kiama, and especially the Nulla Mountain, and the size is smaller than in the type. At Ash Island a rather small stout variety is found, chestnut, with pinkish lip; this inosculates with a variety of *H. Grayi*. The last variety to be mentioned, figured Pl. X., Fig. 5, very dark, granulated and ribbed as usual, with pink lip and livid mouth, does not present any tangible specific difference from the preceding. It is from Ulladulla, collected by Mr. Masters. Although of small dimensions, 0·90, 0·75, 0·50 *of an inch*, the lip is fully formed, the umbilicus perfectly closed, and a thin callous deposit extends between the margin.

93. Helix subgranosa. *Le Guillou*.

Le Guillou, in Revue Zool., 1842, p. 137.
Pfr., Mon. Hel. Viv., Vol. I., p. 83.

Shell sub-globose, umbilicated, thin, pellucid, of a light reddish-brown colour, beneath a dusky white, finely, longitudinally and transversely striated, for the most part granulated; whorls 4, convexly depressed; peristome sharp, angled near the umbilicus, lip straight, dilated above the umbilicus, and broadly reflected.

Diameter 1·10; *height* 0·90 *of an inch.*

Habitat. Northern Australia.—*Le Guillou.*

Not having ever seen this species, the above characters have been taken from Pfeiffer, *Mon. Hel. Viv.*

94. Helix læsa. *Reeve.* Plate II. Fig. 9. M.C.
Reeve, Conc. Icon. sp. 1490.

Shell rather narrowly deeply umbilicated, depressly-globose, plicately striated, and everywhere minutely granulated, livid-greenish, purple stained; spire sub-conoid; whorls 5 to 6, convex, the last a little deflected in front; aperture rotundately-lunar, lip expandidly reflected, white, broadly dilated at the umbilicus.

Diameter, greatest 0·98; *least* 0·59; *height* 0·68 *of an inch.*

Habitat. Dural, near Wiseman's Ferry, Hawkesbury River.—*Cox.* Hunter River.—*Scott.*

Reeve, from whom the above description is taken, observes, that it is a simple minutely granulated species, of a peculiar purple livid or greenish hue, allied to *H. Grayi.*

95. Helix Victoriæ. *Cox.* Plate XII. Fig. 5. Australian Museum.

Shell narrowly umbilicated, depressly-globose, thin, finely plicately striated, uniformly brown, but lighter at the base than above; whorls 5, rather rounded, the last much inflated; spire short, suture impressed; aperture rounded, lip thin, simple, margins approximating, columellar margin at its base only slightly reflected.

Diameter, greatest 0·63; *least* 0·50; *height* 0·45 *of an inch.*

Habitat. Western Port, Victoria.—*Masters.*

96. Helix expeditionis. *Cox.* Plate XVIII. Fig. 12. Australian Museum.

Shell openly umbilicated, globosely-depressed, transversely dilated, thin, transparent, light yellowish-brown; whorls 5½ to 6, the last very large, descending in front, irregularly roughly striated, shining, not granular; aperture lunar-oval, faintly tinged inside, within the peristome, with lilac; lip white, porcellaneous, everted for about ¾ of its extent from the columella, the margin of which is rather broadly expanded, ½ covering the umbilicus.

Diameter, greatest 1·04; *least* 0·90; *height* 0·80 *of an inch.*

Habitat. Tropical Australia.—*Sir Thomas Mitchell.*

97. Helix marcescens. *Cox.* Plate IV. Fig. 5; and Plate XVIII.
Fig. 6, 6 a. M.C.
Cox, Pro. Zool. Soc., 1867.

Shell narrowly and deeply umbilicated, depressly-orbicular, thin, translucent, rather shining, very slightly rugosely striated and under the lens, very finely granulated, horny-yellowish; spire con-

vex, obtuse, suture moderate, margined with a narrow reddish streak; whorls 5, slowly increasing, slightly convex, last roundly convex; aperture lunately-rounded; peristome straight, thin, margins somewhat approaching, columellar margin above dilated and reflected.
Diameter, greatest 0·63; least 0·57; height 0·30 of an inch.
Habitat. Clarence River, about South Grafton (under bark and logs).—*MacGillivray.*

A thin horny semi-transparent shell, like a starved miniature of *H. Grayi*, and to be placed next to *H. aridorum*, a much more globose shell, with a deeply impressed suture. The reddish streak along the suture is not always present.

98. Helix monacha. *Pfr.* Plate XVIII. Fig. 13, *from Pro. Zool. Soc.* M.C.
Pfr., Pro. Zool. Soc., 1859, p. 25. Plate XLIII. Fig. 7.

Shell imperforate, globosely-conical, solid, roughly striated and under the lens, minutely granulated, of a chestnut colour: spire conoidly elevated, rather obtuse; whorls 5½, moderately convex, gradually increasing in size, the last slightly descending in front, obsoletely sub-angled in the middle; aperture for the most part diagonal, rotundately-lunar, livid within, shining; peristome flesh coloured, shortly expanded throughout; margins separated, the columellar margin being expanded at its insertion into a triangular adnate plate.
Diameter, greatest 1·08; least 0·85; height 0·90 of an inch.
Habitat. Ash Island, Hunter River; also Mulgoa, near Penrith, and at the Kurrajong, N.S.W.—*Cox.*

This species is not abundant, and is apt to be confounded with the smaller specimens of *H. coriaria*, and the dark specimens of *H. Grayi.*

99. Helix Mulgoæ. *Cox.* Plate I. Figs. 3, 7, 7 a. M.C.

Shell with a deep almost covered umbilicus, thin, light, transparent, horny, turbinately-globose, generally reddish-brown, Fig. 3, but frequently pale olive-green, Fig. 7; whorls 6, the last much inflated, and obsoletely keeled, descending in front: obliquely, rather roughly striated above the obsolete keel, smooth and shining below; aperture lunately-rounded, light purple within: peristome very slightly thickened; lip a little everted, pale bluish-white; margins approaching, joined by a thin shining callosity; columella white, dilated, almost covering the umbilicus.
Diameter, greatest 1·05; least 0·90; height 1·00 of an inch.
Habitat. Mulgoa, near Penrith, N.S.W.—*Cox.*

At times, after rain, this species is very abundant, otherwise it is not to be found except by digging deeply about the roots of shrubs where it buries itself, and remains for months. There are two very distinct varieties of it—one of a reddish-brown colour, the other of a pale olive-green. This species has for years given me much trouble in determining several of the species of the Australian Land Shells; for a time I considered it as a variety of *H. Grayi*, but, although extremely like varieties of that species, where no red blotch is found round the umbilicus, or following the course of the suture, it is a much thinner, lighter, and less solid shell; but the two species are easily distinguished by the animal, on which more stress should be laid in the determination of species. In hopes of having the species determined, I forwarded to the late Mr. Hugh Cuming, to whom I am indebted for many similar acts of kindness, a number of specimens; the greater number of them were returned to me, labelled *H. monacha* of *Pfr.*, and the others *H. corneo-virens*; but they do not agree with the descriptions of those species as given by Pfeiffer. A number of specimens of a shell lately added to the Australian Museum from Eastern Creek, about 20 miles from Mulgoa, by Mr. Masters, so thoroughly agree with the general characters I have given of this species, *except*, that they have the colouring round the umbilicus, and following the line of suture as in *H. Grayi*, which makes it very doubtful to which species these specimens should be referred.

100. Helix Scotti. *Cox.* Plate X. Fig. 4, 4 a. M.C.
Cox, Catalogue of Australian Land Shells, 1864, p. 36.

Shell narrowly umbilicated, turbinately-globose, radiately-roughly striated, minutely granular throughout, sub-pellucid, chestnut coloured, paler at the apex; whorls 6, slightly convex, the last tumid and rounded; aperture lunately-sub-circular; peristome moderately thickened, straight, partly reflected, white within.

Diameter, greatest 1·50; *least* 1·25; *height* 0·90 *of an inch.*

Habitat. Mount Keera, Wollongong, N.S.W.—*Mrs. Edward Forde.*

Closely allied to the larger specimens of *H. coriaria*, found at the Clarence River Heads.

101. Helix Stutchburyi. *Pfr.* Plate X. Fig 10. M.C.
Pfr., Pro. Zool. Soc., 1856, p. 386.

Shell perforated, depressly-globose, rather thin, smooth, translucent, slightly shining, radiately rugosely ribbed, yellowish-horny, with two spiral red bands—one above the periphery, the other at the suture; spire short, convexly-conoid, obtuse at the apex; whorls 5, slowly increasing, convex, last rounded, slightly descending in front; aperture diagonal, roundly-lunar; peristome simple, thin, margins scarcely converging; columella callus, white, slightly expanded, triangularly dilated above, and ¼ concealing the moderately sized umbilicus.

Diameter, greatest 0·68; *least* 0·60; *height* 0·35 *of an inch.*

Habitat. Drayton Range, Queensland.—*Stutchbury.* Upper Dawson River, Queensland.—*Greenhill.*

Five specimens from the second locality agree so well with Pfeiffer's description, that I do not hesitate to consider them as identical, although I can see none of the "minute granulations under the lens," and no mention is made of the shell being radiately ribbed or marked, as indeed nearly all Australian *Helices* are.

102. Helix Greenhilli. *Cox.* Plate IX. Fig. 1; and Plate XVIII. Fig. 8. M.C.
Cox, Pro. Zool. Soc., 1865.
Jour. de Conchyl., 1865, p. 46.

Shell umbilicated, globosely-turbinated, smooth, obsoletely striated, under the lens are manifested minute undulating lines, closely packed together, reddish-chestnut above, greenish-yellow below; whorls 6, the last very large, convex, the others only slightly convex; aperture lunately-sub-circular; peristome thin, moderately reflected, columellar margin dilated at the base, almost covering the umbilicus: lip white within, greenish-yellow without.

Diameter, greatest 1·20; *least* 1·00; *height* 0·90 *of an inch.*

Habitat. Upper Dawson River, in Queensland.—*Greenhill.*

In general appearance very like *H. pachystyloides*, but at once distinguished from that species, or any other Australian land shell, by the wavy lines of sculpture.

XVIII.—SECTION GALAXIAS. *Pfr.* Vers. p. 134.

* H. pachystyla.	⁕ H. Dunkiensis.	⁕ H. tornus.
* H. prunum.	⁕ H. Forsteriana.	⁕ H. aridorum.
* H. funiculata.	⁕ H. pachystyloides.	⁕ H. pomum.
* H. exocarpi.	⁕ H. carcharias.	⁕ H. perinflata.
⁕ H. plectilis.	⁕ H. corneo-virens.	⁕ H. Duralensis.
⁕ H. leptogramma.	⁕ H. Blackmani.	⁕ H. Macleayi.

103. Helix pomum. *Pfr.* Plate IV. Fig. 7. M.C.
Pfr., Symbolæ, Vol. II., p. 57, 1842.
Helix sphæroidea. *Le Guillou, Revue. Zool.*, 1845, p. 188.
Helix Urvillei. *Hombr. et Jacq., Voy. au Pole Sud.*, Vol. V., p. 1. Pl. 3. Fig. 1—3, 1854.
Reeve, Conc. Icon. sp. 362.

Shell narrowly umbilicated, globular, solid, glossy, obsoletely wrinkled with lines of growth and still more faintly with transverse lines sometimes wanting, covered uniformly with a tawny-yellow epidermis, occasionally reddish, and frequently paler at the base; spire very short, obtuse, suture irregularly crenulated; whorls 4½ to 5, convex, rapidly increasing, the last inflated, suddenly deflected in front, narrowly channeled out near the umbilicus; aperture nearly diagonal, lunately-rounded; peristome white, moderately thickened and slightly everted, the dilated columellar margin with a wide tooth-like enlargement internally, and externally, nearly covering the umbilicus.

Diameter, greatest 1·60; *least* 1·35; *height* 1·00 *of an inch.*

Habitat. Port Essington.—*MacGillivray.* Arnheim's Land, N.W. Australia.—*Cox.*

Representing *H. pachystyla* of the N.E. coast.

104. Helix pachystyla. *Pfr.* Plate VI. Fig. 8. M.C.
Pfr., Pro. Zool. Soc., 1845, p. 71.
Reeve, Conc. Icon. sp. 364.

Shell imperforate, globular, solid, glossy, faintly wrinkled with lines of growth, having finer striæ between, and decussated with still fainter concentric and oblique rugose striæ, covered with reddish-yellowish, or greenish-brown epidermis, generally streaked with brown ; spire very short, obtuse ; suture indistinctly crenulated ; whorls 5 to 5½, convex, rapidly increasing, the last inflated, shortly deflected anteriorly ; aperture nearly diagonal, irregularly lunately-rounded ; peristome white, thickened, slightly reflected, especially at the base, columellar margin expanded, hollowed, nearly straight within, and forming an obsolete broad tooth, externally spread over the umbilicus, edges connected by a callus.

Diameter, greatest 1·80 ; *least* 1·50 ; *height* 1·30 *of an inch.*

Habitat. Facing Isle, Port Curtis, Dunk Isle, Cape Upstart, and Wide Bay.—*MacGillivray.* Port Denison and Rockhampton, Queensland.—*Cox.*

A more ponderous shell than the preceding, which seems peculiar to N.W. Australia, while the present ranges along the whole of the N.E. coast. It is also distinguished by having transverse striæ, and being quite imperforate. I have a very remarkable variety of this species from Miriam Vale, Port Curtis, it is very thin, greenish-olive, and of very small size ; a small mature specimen, the margins of the mouth of which are joined by a callus, measuring not more than 0·95, 0·80, and 0·60 *of an inch.*

105. Helix pachystyloides. *Cox.* Plate V. Fig. 4. M.C.

Shell narrowly and deeply umbilicated, globular, somewhat solid, horny-yellow, rather glossy ; the light wrinkled lines of growth decussated with irregular wrinkles, very closely set together ; spire short, obtuse ; suture irregularly crenulated ; whorls 5, convex, rapidly increasing, last very large, inflated below ; aperture nearly diagonal, irregularly roundly-lunate ; margins slightly approaching, and connected by a thin callus, white lipped, livid within ; peristome flesh-coloured, uniformly curved, expanded outwardly, more so in front, and on the columellar margin, which is dilated above, somewhat callus within and outwardly partially concealing the umbilicus.

Diameter, greatest 1·20 ; *least* 1·00 ; *height* 0·85 *of an inch.*

Habitat. Cape York.—*Daniel.*

Varies considerably in solidity, being sometimes even delicate, thin and horny, it is then most nearly allied to the very small, but exumbilicated variety of *H. pachystyla* alluded to.

106. Helix leptogramma. *Pfr.* Plate XI. Fig. 4. *copied from Reeve.*

Pfr., Pro. Zool. Soc., 1845, p. 127.
Reeve, Conc. Icon. sp. 437.

Shell umbilicated, globose, thin, striated, with close-set concentric, impressed lines, fleshy-white, with three or four narrow red bands ; whorls 4½, rather convex, last inflated, shortly descending in front ; aperture scarcely oblique, roundly-lunate ; peristome white, simple, shortly expanded, margins joined with a diffused very thin callus,

columellar margin much dilated, white, shining, reflected, ½ concealing the narrow umbilicus.
Diameter, greatest 0·67 ; least 0·55 ; height 0·51 of an inch.
Habitat. Cygnet Bay, North Australia.—*Pfeiffer.* South Australia.—*Reeve*—which is undoubtedly a mistake, Mr. G. F. Angas having lately found inside the specimens now in the British Museum a label marked in Lieut. Dring's own handwriting, "Cygnet Bay, N. Australia."
Reeve remarks of this species, that it is a light globose shell, encircled round the middle and upper part with three or four delicately painted brownish-red bands. Its closest affinity is with *H. bitæniata* of South Australia.

107. Helix Forsteriana. *Pfr.* Plate IV. Fig. 8. M.C.
Pfr., Pro. Zool. Soc., 1851.
Reeve, Conc. Icon. sp. 439.
Shell umbilicated, depressly-globose, rather thin, above finely granulated throughout, reddish-brown of various tints, encircled by two pale yellowish bands; spire not much elevated, convexly-conical; whorls 6, slowly increasing, moderately convex, last roundly-convex, descending in front; base convex, smooth, yellowish-white, umbilicus small, deep, a brown spot inside the columella; aperture diagonal, sub-ovately-lunate; peristome simple, straight, margins scarcely approaching, slightly expanded and reflected anteriorly, and more so along the columella which is dilated above.
Diameter, greatest 1·25 ; least 1·10 ; height 0·70 of an inch.
Habitat Islands off the N.E. coast of Australia.—*MacGillivray.*
Although subject to considerable variation in size, distinctness of the bands, and in other respects, this shell does not merge into any other species. It should come next to *H. Grayi*, but it is always a more depressed shell. The largest specimens in my collection are from the Howick Isles, including a beautiful albino variety, which might be mistaken for *H. Dunkiensis*, and the smallest from the Percy Isles, in which last, the depressed form, the granulated surface, the bands and the columellar spot are perfectly distinct.

108. Helix torulus. *Ferussac.* Plate XI. Fig. 5, *copied from Ferussac.*
Ferussac, Hist. Moll. Pl. XXVII. Fig. 3–4.
Shell sub-perforated, globular, white, smooth, surrounded by a small transverse brown band, inflated at the base; whorls 6, convex, narrow; aperture small, roundly-lunate; peristome simple, white, upper margin sub-expanded, reflected, somewhat covering the perforation.
Diameter, greatest 0·60 ; least 0·51 ; height 0·43 of an inch.
Habitat. New Holland.—*Ferussac.*
The description is from Pfeiffer's *Mon. Hel. Viv.*, Vol. I, p. 238. Judging from the figures, the shell appears to partake more of the Polynesian than Australian type. The spire is small, conical, and acute.

109. Helix Dunkiensis. *Forbes.* Plate VIII. Fig 9. Australian Museum.
Forbes, Voy. Rattlesnake, Vol. II., p. 378.
Reeve, Conc. Icon. sp. 756.

Shell umbilicated, depressly-globose, solid, rather glossy, closely striated, minutely granulated, pale yellow; spire convexly-conoid, obtuse: whorls 6, moderately convex, slowly increasing, last suddenly deflected in front, very faintly carinated, rather inflated at the base; aperture diagonal, roundly-lunate, margins slightly approaching, white within; peristome with the basal and columellar margins slightly expanded and reflected, slightly dilated above, and covering ¼ of the deep moderately sized umbilicus.

Diameter, greatest 1·40; *least* 1·15; *height* 0·70 *of an inch.*
Habitat. Dunk Island, North Australia.—*MacGillivray.*

The above description, agreeing with that of Forbes, has been taken from a very fine authentic specimen, presented to the Australian Museum by the original collector. The descriptions of Pfeiffer and Reeve do not agree with each other, although professedly derived from the same source, viz., the Cumingian collection. Reeve's description and figure have certainly not been taken from Dunk Island specimens.

110. Helix prunum. *Ferussac.* Plate IV. Fig 6. Australian Museum.
Ferussac Hist. Moll. Pl. 26. Fig. 7—8.
Reeve, Conc. Icon. sp. 353.
Helix argillacea. *Gray, not Ferussac.*
Helix pelodes. *Pfr., Pro. Zool. Soc.,* 1845, p. 126.

Shell umbilicated, somewhat depressly-globose, rather thin, somewhat shining, finely rugosely striated, and minutely granulated, pale flesh coloured, tinged with pink above; spire short, moderately obtuse; whorls 6, convex, rapidly increasing, last inflated, in front slightly descending; below paler, umbilicus moderate, deep; aperture oblique, lunately-circular, within pearly pink; peristome straight, expanded, margins somewhat approximating, columellar margin much dilated above, and ½ concealing the umbilicus.

Diameter, greatest 1·20; *least* 1·00; *height* 0·70 *of an inch.*
Habitat. Port Essington—on bark of the native tea tree—Melaleuca. —*MacGillivray.*

The preceding description has been taken from two specimens in the Australian Museum, collected by the late Mr. MacGillivray, who informed me that much of the pink or rosy hue had faded during the last sixteen years. Reeve's figure represents this shell, but Ferussac's two most assuredly do not. It agrees with Pfeiffer's description of *H. pelodes,* which he himself has finally merged into *H. prunum.* A shell sent to me by the late Mr. Cuming as "*H. prunum,* Port Essington," and figured Pl. IV., Fig. 4, appears to be *H. argillacea,* Fer., from Timor, where it is abundant. I have never known a specimen of *H. argillacea* yet found on the Australian continent.

111. Helix plectilis. *Benson.* Plate IX. Fig. 17, copied from Reeve.
Benson, Ann. and Mag., Nat. Hist., 1853, p. 29.
Reeve, Conc. Icon. sp. 1162.
Helix paleata. Reeve, Conc. Icon. sp. 1399.

Shell with a nearly covered umbilicus, globose, brownish-white, opaque, strongly wrinkled above with very oblique elevated wrinkles, which are angularly flexuose, and irregular; beneath, towards the umbilicus, marked with radiating, straight, and thinner wrinkles; spire very slightly elevated, apex obtuse; whorls 4, convex, sub-angular, last deflected in front; aperture diagonal, somewhat circular; peristome expanded throughout, slightly reflexed, margins closely approaching, joined by a thin callus, columellar margin vaulted, widely reflected, more or less covering the umbilicus.

Diameter, greatest 0·57; least 0·47; height 0·35 of an inch.

Habitat. Shark Bay and Swan River, Western Australia. *Benson.*

This description is merely a version of that of Pfeiffer *Mon. Hel. Viv.*, Vol. IV., p. 250. Reeve remarks that the crumpled sculpture of this species is quite distinct from anything previously known.

112. Helix aridorum. *Cox.* Plate XI. Fig. 16, 16 a. M.C.
Cox, Pro. Zool. Soc., 1867.

Shell deeply umbilicated, depressly-globose, thin, transparent, slightly shining, radiately rugosely striated and under the lens, very finely granulated, pale yellowish-horny; spire small, widely depressed, apex obtuse, suture deeply impressed; whorls 4½, convex, last very large, rounded, swollen; base paler and smoother; aperture lunately circular; peristome thin, straight, reflected, margins converging, columellar margin moderately dilated at the base, and covering ½ of the umbilicus.

Diameter, greatest 0·55; least 0·45; height 0·30 of an inch.

Habitat. Clarence River, under logs in ironbark ranges, burrowing in dry weather.—*MacGillivray.* Brisbane, Queensland.—*Masters.*

113. Helix exocarpi. *Cox.* Plate II. Fig. 2. M.C.

Shell umbilicated, depressly-orbicular, nearly discoid, solid, obscurely, irregularly and sometimes coarsely striated, everywhere finely granulated, not shining, pale yellowish-brown; spire low, widely-convexly-conical; whorls 5, very gradually increasing, flatly convex, last bluntly angular at the periphery, roundly-convex below, descending in front; base paler and smoother, and less finely granulated than above; aperture diagonal, lunately-rounded; peristome simple, regular, slightly expanded, margins approximating, columellar margin triangularly dilated above, and reflected, partially covering the moderately sized umbilicus.

Diameter, greatest 0·70; least 0·65; height 0·35 of an inch.

Habitat. Cherry Tree Hill, Mudgee and Ryalstone, N.S.W.—*Cox.*

114. Helix carcharias. *Pfr.*
Pfr., Pro. Zool. Soc., 1863, p. 528.
Shell with a nearly covered umbilicus, conoidly-globose, slightly solid, under the lens very minutely granulated, flesh coloured; spire conical, apex smooth and rather obtuse; whorls 5, rather convex, the upper ones irregularly tuberculately-plicate, last ventricose, above more lightly plicate, below radiately striated, white, in front greatly deflected; aperture diagonal, sub-circular; peristome simple, thin, narrowly expanded, margins approximated, columellar margin widely reflected in a vaulted manner over the umbilicus.
Diameter, greatest 0·77; *least* 0·63; *height* 0·55 *of an inch.*
Habitat. Shark Bay, Western Australia.
The preceding description has been entirely taken from the source above quoted, as I have never seen a specimen.

115 Helix perinflata. *Pfr.*
Pfr., Pro. Zool. Soc., 1863, p. 528.
Shell umbilicated, globose, solid, shewing wrinkled lines of growth, decussated by impressed lines descending forwards, pinkish-white; spire convexly-conoid, apex obtuse; whorls 4½, last large, ventricose, below very much inflated, obsoletely marked with spiral striæ, deflexed in front; aperture diagonal, lunately-rounded; peristome briefly expanded, columellar margin dilated, and reflected over the narrow umbilicus.
Diameter, greatest 0·93; *least* 0·79; *height* 0·79 *of an inch.*
Habitat. MacDonnell Ranges, central Australia.—*Waterhouse.*
Allied to *H. pomum.* The description is that of Pfeiffer.

116. Helix Blackmani. *Cox.* Plate XI. Fig. 7, 7 a. Australian Museum.

Shell umbilicated, globosely-turbinate, thin, not shining, everywhere obscurely radiately striated, and, under the lens, minutely granulated, yellowish-horny; spire conical, apex obtuse, suture rather deep; whorls 5, convex, quickly increasing, last very large, inflated, regularly rounded throughout, strongly constricted behind the mouth; aperture diagonal, lunately-roundly-oval; peristome simple, straight, thin, much expanded, white, margins very slightly converging, joined by a very thin callus, collumellar margin expanded above, and ½ concealing the moderately sized umbilicus.
Diameter, greatest 0·65; *least* 0·55; *height* 0·45 *of an inch.*
Habitat. Warroo, Port Curtis, Queensland.—*Blackman.*
The only two specimens I have seen, are in the collection of the Australian Museum, and have a striking resemblance in form to *Dermatocera vitrea.* It may also in some manner be looked upon as connecting such shells as *H. pachystyloides* and *H. aridorum.*

117. Helix Macleayi. *Cox.* Plate VIII. Fig. 3.   M.C.
Cox, Pro. Zool. Soc., 1864.
Shell imperforate, depressly-globose, rather thin, smooth, shining, finely radiately striated, pale yellowish-brown, with a single narrow

dark-purple spiral band, becoming very indistinct towards the end of the last whorl; spire convexly-conical, obtuse; whorls 5, increasing in convexity downwards, last rounded, descending in front; aperture diagonal, lunately-ovate; peristome straight, expanded; columella nearly vertical, dilated, adnate, and completely closing the umbilicus; inner lip dark purple, margins not approaching, joined by a thin dark callus.

Diameter, greatest 1·15; *least* 1·00; *height* 0·65 *of an inch.*

Habitat. Port Denison, Queensland.—*Masters and Reinbird.*

This handsome species, of which several specimens have been found on the trunks of the native fig tree, is one of the many departures from the general Australian type, and bears a western Pacific or Philippine aspect.

118. Helix Duralensis. *Cox.* Plate VIII. Fig. 8, 8 a. M.C.

Shell umbilicated, depressly-turbinate, rather solid, roughly ribbed, especially at the suture, very minutely granulated, dark chestnut, somewhat lighter below; spire short, obtuse; whorls 5, gradually increasing in size, rather convex, the last keeled, rounded in front, a little descending; aperture diagonal, rotundately-lunar, pale rose-colour; peristome simple, straight, very thinly reflexed, columellar margin dilated above, and ½ covering the umbilicus.

Diameter, greatest 0·80; *least* 0·64; *height* 0·58 *of an inch.*

Habitat. Dural, near Wiseman's Ferry, on the Hawkesbury River, N.S.W.—*Cox.*

A miniature representative of *H. coriaria*, especially of those specimens collected by Mr. Masters, at Ulladulla. A variety is sometimes met with of a dull yellow colour, pale below, with a white mouth.

119. Helix funiculata. *Pfr.* Plate XI. Fig. 15. M.C.

Pfr., Pro. Zool. Soc., 1854.
Reeve, Conc. Icon. sp. 1363.

Shell rather largely umbilicated, orbicular, rather swollen, obliquely plicately striated, and rugosely granulated, fulvous-chestnut, encircled with a single pale zone; spire convex, with the suture impressed; whorls 7, rounded, the last somewhat obscurely encircled with a broad obtuse keel; aperture orbicularly-lunar, lip a little reflected, broadly depressed at the columella.

Diameter, greatest 1·00; *least* 0·80; *height* 0·65 *of an inch.*

Habitat. Islands in Torres Straits, North Australia.—*Edwards.*

120. Helix corneo-virens. *Pfr.* Plate XVIII. Fig. 2,
copied from Reeve. M.C.
Pfr., Zeit-schrift für Malac., 1851, p. 25.
Reeve, Conc. Icon. sp. 1366.

Shell with a nearly covered umbilicus, conoidly-globose, thin, somewhat inflated, obliquely rugose at the upper part, smooth beneath, horny-green, sub-diaphanous; spire obtuse; whorls 5 to 6, slightly convex, the last faintly angled, descending in front; aperture obliquely-lunar, rather large, lip thinly reflected, broadly depressed at the columella, lip white.

Diameter, greatest 0·97 ; least 0·73 ; height 0·83 of an inch.
Habitat. Picton and Mulgoa, New South Wales.—*Cox.*

Reeve, from whom this description is taken, states that it is "a light sub-inflated diaphanous horny shell, of simple character." The late Mr. Hugh Cuming was the first to draw my attention to the identity of this species.

XIX.—SECTION PLAGIOPTYCHA. *Pfr.* Vers. p. 135.

* H. duclosiana.

121. Helix duclosiana. *Fer.* Plate XI. Fig. 2, 2 a., *copied from Ferussac.*
Ferussac, Hist. Moll. Pl. 51, A. Fig. 6.
Reeve, Conc. Icon. sp. 761.

Shell umbilicated, depressly-semi-globose, rather thin, very finely obliquely striated, shining, alabaster-white ; spire shortly conoid, apex rather obtuse ; whorls 4½, slightly convex, last somewhat depressed, descending in front, rather flattened at the base ; aperture diagonal, lunately-oval ; peristome simple, margins somewhat approaching, right slightly expanded, basal furnished within with a deep transverse deposit of callus, outwardly forming a white wrinkled mark like a cicatrix, columellar margin dilated above, reflexed, ½ covering the narrow umbilicus.

Diameter, greatest 0·60 ; least 0·51 ; height 0·31 of an inch.
Habitat. New Holland.—*Ferussac.*

I have given Pfeiffer's description of this shell *Mon. Hel. Viv.*, Vol. III., p. 243, which, I think, has been erroneously considered to be Australian. Reeve remarks that it is a semi-transparent white shell, having a tooth-like callosity within the aperture, and no corresponding indentation without. As this forms one of a small and very natural group of shells, the rest of which are known to be West Indian, it seems probable that its true habitat will prove to be some locality nearer Hayti than Australia.

XX.—SECTION PLANISPIRA. *Pfr.* Vers. p. 136.

* H. brevipila.   * H. Porteri.   * H. Hystrix.

122. Helix brevipila. *Pfr.* Plate V. Fig. 2 a., 2 b., *natural size and magnified.* M.C.
Pfr., Pro. Zool. Soc., 1849, p. 130.
Reeve, Conc. Icon. sp. 777.

Shell umbilicated, depressly-globose, thin, translucent, obsoletely rugosely striated, and, under the lens, very finely rugose, covered throughout with short stiff hairs, horny reddish-brown ; spire small, broadly conical, apex acute ; whorls 5, rather convex, last rounded, large, somewhat tumid, deflected in front ; umbilicus narrow ; aperture lunately-oval; peristome white, thin, expanded, reflected, margins approximating, columellar partially concealing the umbilicus.

Diameter, greatest 0·60; *least* 0·50; *height* 0·30 *of an inch*.

Habitat. Widely distributed, from South Australia and Victoria, through New South Wales and Queensland to Cape York; and the Islands in Torres Strait.

From so extensive a geographical range this species might be expected to vary much. Those described are of the largest size, from the Clarence River. But the shell is usually smaller, very thin, shewing under the lens little of any wrinkling of the surface, and having the spire either flat or even submersed. A pretty smooth variety from Cape York has the spire as acute as in those described. In large specimens the pili almost entirely disappear. Those I have from Victoria are unusually dark in colour.

123. Helix Porteri. *Cox.* Plate III. Fig. 6 a., 6 b. M.C.
Cox, Pro. Zool. Soc., 1866, p. 373.

Shell umbilicated, depressly-circular, rather swollen, under the lens obsoletely plicately striated, minutely granulated, and thickly studded with very short hairs, reddish-chestnut; spire small, obtuse; whorls 4½, convex, last swollen, suddenly deflected in front, constricted behind the mouth; aperture roundly-lunate; peristome rather thin, expanded, white, margins approximating, lower border rather straight, columellar margin dilated above and reflected, partially concealing the umbilicus.

Diameter, greatest 0·75; *least* 0·63; *height* 0·50 *of an inch*.

Habitat. Upper Clarence River, at Guy Faux.—*Porter*. Upper Richmond River, at Cowlong, in Cedar brushes under logs.—*MacGillivray*.

This shell bears much general resemblance to specimens of *H. mansueta*, from the Pine Mountain, Lismore, which are darker than Queensland specimens; but the presence of pili, the white lip, the narrower and more covered umbilicus, are very distinctive characters in *H. Porteri*, which is besides closely allied to the more diminutive *H. brevipila*, and occupies a place between it and *H. mansueta*.

124. Helix Hystrix. *Cox.* Plate XVII. Fig. 5, *natural size*,
5 a. *and* 5 b. *magnified*. Australian Museum.

Shell openly umbilicated, discoid, flattened on the top, yellowish-brown, covered with coarse long bristles in regular rows; whorls 5, gradually increasing, rounded, last descending in front, suture deep and narrow; aperture diagonal, rounded; peristome simple, lip everted, columellar margin not dilated.

Diameter, greatest 0·55; *least* 0·44; *height* 0·23 *of an inch*.

Habitat. Port Curtis.—*Cox*.

Unlike any other Australian species, and at once recognised by its discoid form and bristled surface.

XXI.—SECTION HYDRA. *Adams.*

* H. patruelis.   * H. Angasiana.   * H. bizeniata.
* H. Cassandra.   * H. Flindersi.   * H. Evandaleana.
* H. Lincolniensis. * H. Lorioliana. * H. luteo-fusca.

125. Helix patruelis. *Adams and Angas.* Plate III. Fig 8. M.C.
Adams and Angas, Pro. Zool Soc., 1863, p. 520.

Shell umbilicated, orbicularly-depressed, rather coarsely rugosely ribbed, especially at the suture, rather thin, moderately shining, reddish-chestnut, with a pale spiral band under the suture; spire widely and obtusely-conical; whorls 5, convex, last whorl sometimes indistinctly angulated, not descending in front; base smoother and more glossy than above, with a wide yellowish patch surrounding the dark circumference of the umbilicus, which is moderate and deep; aperture diagonal, lunately-ovate; peristome simple, thin, straight, the dark columellar margin dilated above and reflected, to cover ½ of the umbilicus.

Diameter, greatest 1·00; *least* 0·80; *height* 0·50 *of an inch.*
Habitat. Port Lincoln, under dead logs.—*Angas.* Flinders Island.—*Cox.*

A very variable species; an examination of a series collected by Mr. Masters shows the ground colour to range from pale reddish-horny to very dark reddish-chestnut, the band is seldom very well defined, is often very indistinct, and occasionally wanting; and the yellow patch on the base may be indistinct or absent. Two specimens from Flinders Island are of a smaller variety; but there can be no doubt as to specific identity, for one shows very plainly, not merely, in addition to similarity of sculpturing, &c., the pale patch on the lower surface, but also the spiral band below the suture.

126. Helix Angasiana. *Pfr.* Plate VI. Fig. 4.   M.C.
Pfr., Journ. de Conchyl., 1862, p. 228. Pl. X. Fig. 2.

Shell perforated, globularly-conical, solid, porcellaneous, shining, white, under the lens closely and irregularly obsoletely rugosely striated, giving a granular feel to the touch, and more obsoletely decussated with spiral lines; spire conoid, obtuse; whorls 5, convex, last descending in front, very large, inflated; aperture moderately oblique, nearly round; peristome straight, smoothly thickened and expanded, especially on the columellar margin where it nearly conceals the umbilicus.

Diameter, greatest 0·85; *least* 0·75; *height* 0·70 *of an inch.*
Habitat. Darling River, New South Wales.—*Masters.*

This singular, smooth, white, porcellaneous shell, without any coloured markings whatever, corresponds exactly with the original description and figures by Pfeiffer, quoted above. The colour was stated to be "whitish?" It is probable that it was a very old shell, from its extensive deposit of callous matter. Subsequently, in the *Journ. de Conchyl.*, 1863, p. 275, M. Crosse remarks that an examination of two living specimens shows that the diagnosis should be modified, the individual figured having lost all its colours. In this he is mistaken—the coloration he gives agrees very well with that of an extensive series of specimens in my possession of the next species; but not one of those coloured ones has the outer lip more than very faintly *thickened and reflected*, as stated by Angas, *Pro. Zool. Soc.*, 1863, p. 520, to be the case with his—nor have any of those, upwards of 100 in number, collected lately by Mr. Masters. While not desirous to add to the number of doubtful species, I cannot admit that the thin, brightly banded, conspicuously striately ribbed specimens to be next described, as specifically identical with this massive, smooth, porcellaneous, granular, white shell already distinguished, and I therefore make it a new species. Pfeiffer's original is stated by him to be from the neighbourhood of Lake Torrens, in 29° S. latitude. Angas gives "under salt bushes, on the plains at Arrowie, near Lake Torrens."

127. Helix bitæniata. *Cox.* Plate IV. Fig. 9. M.C.
H. Angasiana, not of Pfeiffer. *Crosse, Journ. de Conchyl.*, 1863, p. 275.
Angas, Pro. Zool. Soc., 1863, p. 520.

Shell perforated, globularly-conical, thin, translucent, slightly glossy, rather strongly rugosely and somewhat plicately striated, more so at the suture, horny-reddish-yellow, sometimes tinged with green, with two spiral bands of purplish-chestnut on each whorl, one under the suture, the other along the middle; spire obtusely-conical; whorls 5, convex, last inflated, not descending in front; base convex, pale yellowish-horny, umbilicus small, $\frac{1}{2}$ covered; aperture ovately-lunar; peristome straight, very slightly thickened and expanded, right and outer border regularly curved, columellar margin forming a blunt angle, and then slanting upwards, dilated and reflected, very moderately callous, white or pinkish, as is also in the interior of the mouth.

Diameter, greatest 0·70; *least* 0·65; *height* 0·50 *of an inch.*
Habitat. Port Augusta, South Australia.—*Masters.*

Enough has already been stated regarding the specific distinctness of this shell and *H. Angasiana*. The name indicates the chief, perhaps the only, character by which it may readily be known from *H. leptogramma*, and yet occasionally the bands are nearly obsolete.

128. Helix Cassandra. *Pfr.*
Pfr., Pro. Zool. Soc., 1863, p. 527.

Shell moderately umbilicated, globosely-depressed, thin, finely striated, and very minutely granulated, hardly shining, above pale brownish-yellow, obsoletely marked with some deeper bands, beneath whitish; spire shortly conically-elevated, with a minute vertex; whorls 5, regularly increasing, the uppermost scarcely at all convex, last inflated, scarcely deflected in front; aperture roundly-lunate, somewhat pearly within; peristome simple, thin, right margin straight, basal slightly reflected, dilated at the umbilicus into a vaulted triangular plate.

Diameter, greatest 1·02; *least* 0·86; *height* 0·59 *of an inch.*

Habitat. Lower Murray River, S. Australia, in bushy patches amongst sandstone cliffs.—*Angas.*

I have taken Pfeiffer's description. *Adams* and *Angas* remark of this shell, that "it is a delicate pale-brown and whitish banded species, somewhat depressed in form, with the outer lip but slightly reflected."

129. Helix Flindersi. *Adams and Angas.*
Adams and Angas, Pro. Zool. Soc., 1863, p. 521.

Shell globosely-conoid, rather thin, moderately umbilicated, brownish-white; whorls 4½, rather convex, rugosely striated, last large, inflated; aperture lunately-ovate, lip callous, partially covering the umbilicus.

Length 7; *breadth* 7 *lines.*

Habitat. Tillowie, near the western slopes of Flinder's Range, South Australia.—*Angas.*

Mr. Angas, from whose description the preceding has been taken, further says that "this remarkably compact and globose species, of which only two specimens have hitherto been found, is characterised by the rugose striæ of the whorls, and by its conoidal spire."

130. Helix Evandaleana. *Pfr.* Plate IX. Fig. 18, 18 a. *enlarged.* M.C.
Pfr., Pro. Zool. Soc., 1863, p. 528.

Shell umbilicated, depressed, rather thin, rugosely-striated, and under the lens granulated and furnished with short hairs, dirty-yellowish or blackish-brown; spire slightly elevated, obtuse, suture rather deep; whorls 4, convex, last more or less obtusely carinated; base convex, the striæ and granulations gradually becoming fainter; umbilicus moderate, deep; aperture lunately-ovate; peristome simple, thin, more or less angular externally, at the columella triangularly dilated above.

Diameter, greatest 0·55; *least* 0·47; *height* 0·30 *of an inch.*

Habitat. Evandale, under dead logs.—*Angas.* Barrier Ranges, S. Australia.—*Masters.*

I have not seen in any other species the same kind of rugose striation, granulation, and pilosity, the last often obsolete, which seems to be characteristic. Angas speaks of a "large umbilicus," while Pfeiffer writes of the same shell "subangusto umbilicata."

131. Helix Lincolniensis. *Pfr.* Plate VI. Fig. 9. M.C.
Pfr., Pro. Zool. Soc., 1863, p. 527.

Shell umbilicated, somewhat conoidly-depressed, rather thin and moderately glossy, pellucid, very closely, coarsely and irregularly rugosely striated, and finely granulated, of a rich deep-chestnut throughout; spire slightly elevated, widely conical, obtuse, suture pale; whorls 5, rather flattened, last rounded, rather depressed above, and sometimes indistinctly angular at the periphery, descending in front; base less strongly striated than above, smoother and more glossy, umbilicus small; aperture lunately-ovate; peristome simple, thin,

straight, margins moderately approximating, columellar margin rather widely expanded above, and reflected over ½ of the umbilicus.
Diameter, greatest 0·80; *least* 0·70; *height* 0·35 *of an inch.*
Habitat. Port Lincoln, S. Australia.—*Angas and Masters.*
My specimens do not vary materially in any respect.

132. Helix Lorioliana. *Crosse.* Plate III. Fig. 4 a, 4 b. M.C.
Crosse, Journ. de Conchyl., 1863, p. 273. Pl. IX. Fig. 6.
Shell perforate, depressly-globose, rather thin, smooth, moderately shining, rugosely striated, especially at the suture, pale reddish-yellow, surrounded with two reddish-chestnut bands, one on the periphery, the other under the suture; spire moderate, depressly and broadly-convex; whorls 5, moderately convex, last convex, rather dilated towards the mouth, descending in front; base smooth, shining, of a paler yellow than above, and more glossy, umbilicus nearly covered; aperture extremely oblique with a horizontal tendency, white within, shewing the two bands; peristome simple, thin, expanded, margins rather approximating, columellar margin thinly, broadly, and triangularly expanded above, tinged with rose colour, and reflected, so as nearly to conceal the umbilicus.
Diameter, greatest 1·05; *least* 0·95; *height* 0·60 *of an inch.*
Habitat. Flinder's Range, S. Australia, in ravines on its western slopes.—*Angas.*

Angas remarks of this, that it is the largest S. Australian land shell yet discovered, of a yellowish-horn colour, banded with orange-brown. The preceding description has been taken from a series of beautiful specimens collected on Flinder's Range by Mr. Masters, not one of which agrees precisely with the figure and description of Crosse, probably taken from a single specimen. His shell is very much more globose, and it is described as imperforate, while in none that I have seen has the umbilicus been covered over.

133. Helix luteo-fusca. *Cox.* Plate XII. Fig 1, and 1 a. Australian Museum.
Shell openly umbilicated, depressed, obliquely rugosely striated, and obsoletely granulated, thin, yellowish-brown or dark chestnut; spire rather prominent; whorls 4½, regularly increasing, last whorl depressed throughout, on which the elevation of the spire depends, periphery blunt, slightly angled, base convex; aperture diagonal, lunately-rounded; peristome simple, lip thin, margins approaching, columellar margin but little everted, the opposite margin inserted beneath the angulation of the second whorl.
Diameter, greatest 0·65; *least* 0·50; *height* 0·33 *of an inch.*
Habitat. Flinder's Range, S. Australia.—*Masters.*

XXII.—SECTION MACROCYCLIS. *Pfr.* Vers. p. 137.

* H. Cunninghami. * H. Mühlfeldtiana.

134. Helix Cunninghami. *Gray.* Plate I. Fig. 5, 5 a. M.C.
Gray, Pro. Zool. Soc., 1834, p. 64.
Griffiths, Animal Kingdom. Pl. XXXVI. Fig. 4.
Reeve, Conc. Icon. sp. 363.
Shell umbilicated, very much depressed, discoid, solid, rugosely

striated, more or less decussated with spiral lines, banded with dark brown and yellow; spire very slightly prominent; whorls 4 to 5, quickly increasing, slightly convex, last very wide, very bluntly keeled, convex above, dilated and obliquely produced, and in front suddenly deflected; below more shining than above, of a deep brownish-black from the periphery to the centre of last whorl, then reddish-yellow to the bottom of the extremely wide and perspective umbilicus; aperture nearly horizontal, transversely lunately-oval; peristome purplish-black within, thickened, reflected, margins approximating and joined with a callus, right slightly curved, anterior rather more so, columellar margin nearly straight, thickened above with a callus.

Diameter, greatest 2·60; least 2·00; height 0·80 of an inch.

Habitat. Brisbane, Wide Bay, Port Curtis, and Rockhampton, Queensland.—*Cox*.

Of this very remarkable shell the preceding description applies to what may be considered as the type, but it is extremely variable. In size, my largest specimen measures 2·80, and my smallest (adult) 1·90 inches, in greatest diameter. The lip may be altogether white, Fig. 5, or purplish-black, Fig. 5 a., or in fact of various tints between white and purplish-black. Some enormous specimens from Port Curtis are of a green colour as the prevailing hue, Fig 5, and then have the lip very greatly thickened and reflected, with a copious callous deposit between the margins. A series of specimens of a small variety from Rockhampton, shew below a similar appearance to that in the description, but above, the bands, mostly narrow, are very numerous and decided.

135. Helix Muhlfeldtiana. *Pfr.* Plate VI. Fig. 2. M.C.

Pfr., *Pro. Zool. Soc.*, 1851.
H. rotabilis. *Reeve, Conc. Icon.* sp. 361.

Shell umbilicated, very much depressed, discoid, solid, scarcely shining, rugosely striated, decussated by very indistinct spiral wrinkled lines, blackish-chestnut, with obscure traces of bands; spire scarcely projecting and sometimes flat; whorls 5, rapidly increasing, very slightly convex, last very wide, swollen, obliquely produced, and suddenly deflected in front, bluntly keeled for one-half its length; below coloured as above, umbilicus very wide and perspective; aperture nearly horizontal, transversely ovately-lunar, margined within with glossy dark purplish-black, with bluish interior; peristome simple, not thickened or reflected except on the columella, margins approaching, connected by a callus, right arcuate, left nearly straight, thickened and very slightly reflected above.

Diameter, greatest 2·50; least 1·85; height 0·70 of an inch.

Habitat. Richmond River.—*MacGillivray*.

Closely allied to the preceding species, but is smaller, and of a dull generally uniform hue, with the lip thin.

XXIII.—SECTION AMPELITA. *Pfr.* Vers. p. 137.

* H. leucocheilus.

136. Helix leucocheilus. *Cox.* Plate VIII. Fig. 7, 7 a, 7 b. M.C.
Helix Mariæ. *Cox, Pro. Zool. Soc.*, 1864, p. 593.

Shell umbilicated, depressly-orbicular, nearly discoid, solid, pellucid, obsoletely radiately striated, under the lens, on both sides, minutely granulated, colour varying between dirty-yellow and pale-chestnut; a reddish or chestnut spiral band above the keel, and another along the suture, with a broad chestnut ring surrounding the umbilicus, which is pale within; spire slightly convex; whorls 5, rather flattened, last keeled behind, remainder convexly-rounded; aperture subquadrately-ovate; peristome white, lipped within, expanded, columella very slightly expanded, and concealing a very small portion of the umbilicus, which is pervious and moderate.

Diameter, greatest 0·65; *least* 0·57; *height* 0·30 *of an inch.*
Habitat. Clarence and Richmond Rivers, N. S. W.—*MacGillivray.*
Brisbane, Queensland.—*Brazier.*

Among the few varieties there is one of a reddish-chestnut colour without bands, Fig. 7 a.

XXIV.—SECTION CAMÆNA. *Pfr.* Vers. p. 138.

* H. bipartita.	* H. semicastanea.	* H. similaris.
* H. Incei.	* H. Yulei.	* H. mansueta.
* H. Lessoni.	* H. Blomfieldi.	* H. mucida.
* H. appendiculata.	* H. cerata.	* H. pliculosa.
* H. Curtisiana.	* H. murina.	* H. morosa.

137. Helix bipartita. *Fer.* Plate V. Fig. 7. M.C.
Fer., Hist. Pl. LXXV. A. Fig. 1.
Reeve, Conch. Icon. sp. 359.

Shell umbilicated, globose, inflated, solid, irregularly striated, under the lens minutely granulated, reddish-yellow, with a narrow reddish-chestnut band under the suture, body whorl, below the periphery, dark purplish-chestnut; spire semi-globular, suture crenulated; whorls 7, slightly convex, last descending in front; aperture diagonal, ovately-lunar, white within; peristome white, expanded and reflected, margins rather approaching and joined with a very thin callus.

Diameter, greatest 2·60; *least* 2·00; *height* 1·70 *of an inch.*
Habitat. Cape York, Albany Island, Cape Direction, N. E. Australia.—*MacGillivray.*

This species varies much in colour. Some of my specimens, of a pale-yellowish hue, have the lower half of the body whorl scarcely a shade darker than the upper portion.

138. Helix Incei. *Pfr.* Plate V. Fig. 5. Plate XVIII. Fig 1. M.C.
Pfr., Pro. Zool. Soc., 1845, p. 126.
Reeve, Conc. Icon. sp. 356.

Shell umbilicated, depressly-globose, very finely striated, with numerous spiral lines and yellow bands of reddish-chestnut and black; spire convexly-conoid; whorls 6, slightly convex, last rounded, rather suddenly deflected in front; mouth diagonally ovately-lunate, white within, shewing the bands; peristome straight, slightly thickened, moderately expanded, but scarcely reflected, margins slightly approximating, columellar margin purplish and triangularly dilated above, reflected, and nearly covering the umbilicus.

Diameter, greatest 1·25; *least* 1·00; *height* 0·70 *of an inch.*

Habitat. Ipswich, Port Curtis, Port Denison, Cape Upstart, Upper Mary and Upper Dawson Rivers, and other localities in Queensland.—*Cox.*

The description applies to the most prevalent form of the shell as figured. It is, however, subject to considerable variation. In some localities it becomes much larger and more solid than usual, when it corresponds with the description of Pfeiffer, *Mon. Hel. Viv.*, Vol. I., p. 329, and resembles the figures of Reeve, who also gives a variety of uniform fulvous-brown, without bands. There is another curious one, which Pfeiffer calls *var β.*, and of which I possess specimens, chestnut, with the bands indistinct, and the last whorl yellow at the base. Plate XVIII., Fig 1, represents a large thin variety numerously and finely banded, from Wide Bay. In fact, among its variations there are some so closely connecting it with *H. Lessoni* as to render it difficult to separate them. On the other hand, its affinities with *H. Yulei* are very obvious.

139. Helix Lessoni. *Pfr.* Plate IV. Fig 10. M.C.

Pfr., Symbolæ, Vol. III., p. 71.

Helix gulosa. *Gould, Exped. Shells,* 1846, p. 17, according to *Pfeiffer.*
Reeve, *Conc. Icon.* sp. 754.

H. seminigra. *Crosse, Journ. de Conchyl,* 1864, p. 289.

Shell perforated, globular, very finely closely striated, rather solid, blackish-chestnut, pale towards the apex, and sometimes spirally lined; spire obtusely-conical or nearly convex, suture pale; whorls 6, slightly convex, last inflated, deflected in front; base convex, frequently shewing traces of spiral lines and bands, especially within the mouth; aperture diagonal, roundly to ovately-lunate, of a shining livid hue within; peristome expanded throughout, rather thickened, white, margins slightly approaching, columellar margin above dilated and reflected, so as partially, sometimes almost entirely, to cover the umbilicus.

Diameter, greatest 1·45; *least* 1·30; *height* 1·00 *of an inch.*

Habitat. Port Curtis, Queensland.—*Cox.*

A variable shell, usually to be recognised at once among its allies by its comparatively small size, the dimensions given above are from an unusually large specimen, its dark, nearly black, unbanded lower portion, and its pale narrowly banded spire, and white lip. Some small specimens of *H. appendiculata* approach it very closely. I have not the slightest hesitation in referring *H. seminigra* of Crosse to this species. It is scarcely even a variety. Specimens from

Miriam Vale, Port Curtis, Queensland, agree in all respects with the published description and measurements.

140. Helix appendiculata. *Pfr.* Plate V. Fig. 11. M.C.
Pfr., Pro. Zool. Soc., 1854, p. 149.
Reeve, Conc. Icon. sp. 1353.

Shell umbilicated, globosely-turbinated, slightly solid, very finely obliquely striated, and, under the lens, covered with extremely faint short minute lines, giving the appearance of lengthened granules, reddish-yellow, spirally banded and lineated with deep chestnut, darker about the mouth; spire broadly-conoid, obtuse; whorls 6, slightly convex, last convex, above strongly deflected in front; base marked as above, umbilicus deep, nearly covered; aperture diagonal, ovately-lunate, white within, then purplish; peristome simple, white or purplish, straight, margins somewhat converging, right expanded, basal reflected, columellar margin above broadly dilated and reflected at the umbilicus, which it nearly conceals.

Diameter, greatest 1·50; *least* 1·25; *height* 0·85 *of an inch.*
Habitat. Port Denison, Queensland.—*Masters.*

This, which is a beautiful representative of the larger, more solid, black lipped, and ex-umbilicated *H. Fraseri*, is generally banded in a precisely similar manner to that species. It has, however, equally close affinities with *H. Lessoni*, evident only after examination of a large series of specimens.

141. Helix semicastanea. *Pfr.* Plate V. Fig. 10. M.C.
Pfr., Zeit-schrift für Malac., 1849, p. 77.
Helix bipartita. Var. *Desh. in Fer. Hist.* Pl. CVII. A. F. 16, 17.
Helix Janellei. *Le Guillou. Revue. Zool.*, 1842, p. 137.
Helix bipartita? *Fer., Hombr. and Jacq. Voy. au Pole Sud. Zool.*,
Vol V., p. 3. Pl. III. Fig. 7—9, 1854.
Reeve, Conc. Icon. sp. 1348.

Shell umbilicated, turbinately-globose, striated, under the lens minutely granulated, somewhat glossy, translucent, above reddish-yellow, base below periphery of body whorl deep chestnut; spire depressly-conoid; whorls 6, slowly increasing, slightly convex, last deflected in front; aperture roundly-lunate, white within, thickened with a callus, expanded, and on anterior and columellar lips reflected, above concealing ½ of the umbilicus.

Diameter, greatest 1·65; *least* 1·40; *height* 1·00 *of an inch.*
Habitat. Islands of N.E. coast of Australia and Torres Strait, from Lizard Island to Stephen's Island.

This species, unquestionably a modified *H. bipartita*, is so variable that a dozen well marked varieties might easily be selected from among the hundreds of specimens now before me. I have taken the preceding description from a Lizard Island specimen. On the peak of that island, the late Mr. MacGillivray found very large and thin specimens under stones, and on the lower grounds, in the scrubs, about the roots of trees, and among dead leaves, a smaller, stouter, and brightly coloured but variable form was abundant; while on a mound-like rocky islet, distant from the shore a couple of hundred yards, a small, dull, solid variety, not exceeding an inch in diameter, but undeniably specifically identical, was met with. A pale band round the periphery is very often present, and marks the division between the upper light and the lower dark portions of the shell. Yet this may be wanting, there being no line of demarcation, the whole surface being yellowish-white. And as a contrast to these last, some specimens are throughout of a dark-chestnut. The difference in size is very great; my smallest specimen, fully formed, is less than an inch in diameter. *H. funiculata*, described elsewhere, I would refer to this head without hesitation; a specimen before me, picked out from a number collected on Stephen's Island, agrees with the descriptions of Pfeiffer and Reeve, and the figure of the latter; it is of a fulvous chestnut colour, encircled with a single pale zone.

142. Helix Yulei. *Forbes.* Plate V. Fig. 3. M.C.
Forbes, Voy. Rattlesnake, Vol. II., p. 377. Pl. II. Fig. 6.
Reeve, Conc. Icon. sp. 1147.

Shell umbilicated, depressly-globose, obliquely finely striated, fulvous, ornamented with broad blackish zones: spire sub-conoid, rather obtuse at the apex; whorls 5, rather convex, the last descending in front, rounded at the periphery, rather flat at the base; umbilicus funnel shaped, dark-chestnut; aperture almost diagonal, lunately sub-circular, lip black, margins approximating, broadly expanded, columellar margin dilated.

Diameter, greatest 1·36; *least* 1·10; *height* 0·87 *of an inch.*

Habitat. Port Molle, and Islands off Port Denison, Queensland.—*MacGillivray.*

I have adopted Pfeiffer's description, *Mon. Hel. Viv.*, Vol. III., p. 224, as Reeve has done, because it has been taken from the typical specimen described by Forbes. My own, from Port Denison, are paler than in Reeve's figure, but still have a decided fulvous tinge in some cases; the number of dark chestnut spiral lines and bands varies from 4 to 8. The black lip and umbilical patch afford distinctive characters between this and *H. Incei*, to which it is most intimately allied.

143. Helix Blomfieldi. *Cox.* Plate I. Fig. 1. M.C.
Cox, Catalogue of Australian Land Shells, p. 19, 1864.

Shell imperforate, solid, globosely-conical, very finely closely striated, deep purplish-chestnut on body whorl, the second generally very much lighter, and the remainder reddish-yellow, these last usually have a few very inconspicuous spiral coloured lines or bands, and obsolete microscopic spiral lines; spire large, very gradually-conical, blunt, suture margined below with yellow; whorls 6, rather convex, 2nd large, 3rd very large, inflated, much produced, slightly convex above to the periphery; aperture diagonal, ovately lunate, within glossy, of a purplish-leaden hue; peristome straight, everywhere expanded, and reflected, margins joined by a thin callus, columellar margin

expanded over the umbilicus, by which it is at length completely hidden.
Diameter, greatest 1·80; *least* 1·30; *height* 1·20 *of an inch.*
Habitat. Miriam Vale, Port Curtis, Queensland.—*Blomfield.*
The nearest approach to this species is made by the uniformly dark variety of *H. Frazeri*, mentioned under its proper head. But this is remarkable for its unusual elongation above and below, giving it something of a Bulimoid appearance.

144. Helix cerata. *Cox.* Plate VIII. Fig. 4. M.C.
H. Forbesi. *Cox, Pro. Zool. Soc.,* 1864, p. 40.
H. corea. *Cox, Catalogue of Australian Land Shells,* p. 36, 1864.

Shell imperforate, solid, globosely-conical, rather glossy, finely striated, very pale waxy-yellow, with numerous spiral reddish lines, and very narrow bands; spire rather large, broadly-conical, obtuse; whorls 7, rather convex, last very large, dilated and produced in front, above deflected; aperture diagonal, ovately-lunate, white within; peristome straight, everywhere expanded and slightly reflected, margins scarcely approximating, joined by a callus; columella thickened and expanded, completely obliterating the umbilicus.
Diameter, greatest 1·60; *least* 1·25; *height* 1·10 *of an inch.*
Habitat. Port Molle and Port Denison, Queensland.—*Masters.*
A very remarkable shell, in form and solidity approaching *H. Blomfieldi*, and in colour and markings *H. Incei*. In short the wonderful parallelism of these shells is so obvious that it may be set down as *H. cerata* is to *H. Incei*, so is *H. Blomfieldi* to *H. Lessoni*. The ground colour is white; the epidermis is remarkably thin. The shell has a waxy and smooth, rather glossy appearance, especially below.

145. Helix Curtisiana. *Pfr.*
Pfr., *Pro. Zool. Soc.,* 1863, p. 528.

Shell narrowly umbilicated, conoidly-semi-globose, solid, striated, chestnut; spire conoidly-convex, above whitish, apex rather obtuse; suture with a white thread; whorls 6, slowly increasing, last large, convex, somewhat angular above the middle, flattish at the base, descending in front; aperture nearly diagonal, roundly-lunate; peristome scarcely thickened, narrowly expanded, columellar margin triangularly dilated above.
Diameter, greatest 1·14; *least* 0·98; *height* 0·67 *of an inch.*
Habitat. Port Curtis.—*Angas.*
This description has been translated from Pfeiffer, who indicates the position of the shell to be next *H. Yulei.*

146. Helix similaris. *Fer.* Plate IX. Fig. 14. M.C.
Fer., *Hist. Moll.* Pl. XXV. B. Fig. 1—4; and Pl. XXVII. A. Fig. 3.
Reeve, *Conc. Icon.* sp. 149.

Shell umbilicated, depressly-globose, scarcely shining, rather thin, translucent, striated, pale yellowish-horny, with, usually, a narrow reddish band; spire obtusely-conical; whorls convex, last slightly

descending in front; aperture roundly-lunate, diagonal; peristome white within, straight, slightly expanded and reflected; columella dilated above and ½ covering the moderately sized and pervious umbilicus.
Diameter, greatest 0·65 ; *least* 0·50 ; *height* 0·30 *of an inch.*
Habitat. Frankland Isles, N.E. coast of Australia.—*MacGillivray.* Double Bay, Sydney, N.S.W., in gardens.—*Cox.*
In the last mentioned locality, where Mrs. Forde first observed it as a novelty, it occurred in Mr. Guilfoyle's nursery, and was doubtless an importation among soil with plants. With reference to the locality on the Frankland Isles, the late Professor E. Forbes suggested that it might have been carried thither by floating timber, which is extremely probable. It is pre-eminently a wanderer, as will be seen by the list of places, widely separated, where it has been found :— Cuba, Brazil, Reunion, Mauritius, Natal, Java, Bengal, China, Sandwich Islands.

147. Helix mansueta. *Pfr.* Plate II. Fig. 1. M.C.
Pfr., Pro. Zool. Soc., 1854, p. 57.
Reeve, Conc. Icon. sp. 1304.

Shell umbilicated, orbicularly-depressed, rather thin, diaphanous, very closely but almost obsoletely striated and under the lens, minutely granulated, without lustre, deep vinous-chestnut; spire short, broadly-conical, rather acute at the apex, suture impressed; whorls 5, convex, very gradually increasing, last nearly descending in front, rounded; umbilicus moderate, perspective; aperture diagonal, lunately-oval; peristome usually pale or coloured, not thickened, very briefly expanded, margins rather approximating, columellar margin slightly triangularly dilated above and reflected.
Diameter, greatest 0·70 ; *least* 0·55 ; *height* 0·30 *of an inch.*
Habitat. Moreton Bay, Queensland.—*Masters.* Richmond River, N.S.W.—*MacGillivray.*
Perhaps the descriptions of Pfeiffer and Reeve, which frequently disagree, were taken from a single specimen. None of mine shew any angularity on the periphery as stated by them, but not shown on Reeve's figure, nor are there either pale or dark markings about the umbilicus, as mentioned by these writers. All the specimens which I have seen are concolorous, and of a vinous hue.

148. Helix mucida. *Pfr.*
Pfr., Pro. Zool. Soc., 1856, p. 329.

Shell umbilicated, turbinately-depressed, rather thin, finely striated, deep red, appearing as if spread over with mould; spire conoid, rather blunt; whorls 5, convex, gradually increasing, last rounded, descending in front, sub-angular around the funnel-shaped umbilicus; aperture nearly diagonal, roundly lunar, shining flesh-colour within; peristome briefly expanded, margins scarcely converging, columellar margin triangularly dilated above and spreading.
Diameter, greatest 0·79 ; *least* 0·65 ; *height* 0·43 *of an inch.*
Habitat. Percy Isles, N. E. Coast of Australia.—*Chimmo.*

A variety of smaller dimensions is alluded to by Pfeiffer, from whom the preceding has been entirely taken, *Mon. Hel. Viv.*, Vol. IV., p. 264. Doubtless a very remarkable and easily distinguished species, from its deep red colour and "mouldy" appearance.

149. Helix pliculosa. *Pfr.* Plate IX. Fig. 12. M.C.
Pfr., Pro. Zool. Soc., 1856, p. 386.

Shell umbilicated, turbinately-globose, delicately thin, above closely covered with little folds, diaphanous, slightly shining, reddish-horny; spire conoid, apex fine; whorls 5, slightly convex, last sub-angular above the middle, rounded in front, scarcely descending, inflated at the base, somewhat compressed about the moderate, pervious umbilicus; aperture oblique, lunately-rounded; peristome white, margins somewhat converging, right slightly expanded, columellar margin dilated above, reflected, and forming with the basal an obtuse angle.

Diameter, greatest 0·63; *least* 0·51; *height* 0·39 *of an inch*.

Habitat. Drayton Range, Queensland.—*Stutchbury*. Rockhampton.—*Cox*.

I have adopted Pfeiffer's description with very slight alteration, as the only specimen in my cabinet is not in very good condition. Although this shell may be associated with *H. aridorum* and *H. marcescens*, it is not granulated.

150. Helix murina. *Pfr.*
Pfr., Pro. Zool. Soc., 1856, p. 384.

Shell umbilicated, turbinately-globose, thin, regularly striated, granular, somewhat roughened, deep red; spire shortly conoid, slightly obtuse; whorls nearly 5, convex, last inflated, scarcely descending in front, somewhat compressed about the moderate, pervious umbilicus; aperture diagonal, lunately-rounded, pearly within; peristome brownish, fleshy, everywhere shortly expanded, margins somewhat converging, columellar margin dilated above, reflected in a vaulted manner.

Diameter, greatest 0·60; *least* 0·47; *height* 0·35 *of an inch*.

Var. β. Paler, brownish-horny, with white peristome.

Habitat. Admiralty Islands. Var. β. Northern Australia.—*Stutchbury*.

The preceding has been entirely derived from Pfeiffer, *Mon. Hel. Viv.*, Vol. IV., p. 267.

151. Helix morosa. *Morelet*.
Morelet, in Journ. de Conchyl., 1853-4, p. 369. Plate XI. Fig. 15.

Shell with covered umbilicus, turbinately-globose, depressed, thin, plicately striated, granulated under the lens, of a uniform dark-chestnut colour; spire conoidly-depressed; whorls 6, somewhat convex, gradually increasing in size, the last not descending, base almost flat; aperture oval, of a uniform colour; peristome scarcely thickened, shortly reflected, of a violet tint, margins joined by a

callus, columellar margin dilated into a triangular plate concealing the umbilicus.
Diameter, greatest 1·22 ; *least* 1·12 ; *height* 0·78 *of an inch.*
Habitat. Moreton Bay, Queensland.—*Morelet.*

XXV.—SECTION VALLONIA. *Pfr.* VERS. p. 139.

* H. cyclostomata.   * H. Delessertiana.   ♀ H. Alexandræ.

152. Helix cyclostomata. *Le Guillou.* Plate X. Fig. 12, *natural size and magnified.* M.C.
Le Guillou, Revue. Zool., 1842, p. 141.
Helix Tuckeri. *Pfr., Symbolæ*, Vol. III., p. 77, 1846.
Helix strangulata. *Homb. et Jacq., Voy. au Pole Sud., Zool.*, Vol. V., p. 16, 1854. Plate VI. Fig. 1—4.

Shell umbilicated, depressed, thin, slightly shining, pellucid, faintly striated, and sparingly covered with very short hairs, brownish-horny, occasionally with an obscure reddish line ; spire slightly elevated ; whorls 4, flattish, last bulging and turned down in front, constricted behind the aperture ; base convex, umbilicus moderate, open ; aperture diagonal, somewhat circular ; peristome white within, slightly thickened and reflected, the margins approaching.
Diameter, greatest 0·40 ; *least* 0·32 ; *height* 0·15 *of an inch.*
Habitat. Queensland, from Brisbane to Cape York, both near the coast and inland ; also in the islands of Torres Strait.—*Cox.* Dr. Mueller has even sent me specimens from St. Kilda, near Melbourne.

153. Helix Delessertiana. *Le Guillou.* Plate V. Figs. 8 a., 8 b.   M.C.
Le Guillou, Revue. Zool., 1842, p. 138.
Helix Taranaki. *Gray, M.S.S., in Pfr.'s Symbolæ*, Vol. III., p. 19, 1846.
Helix Torresiana. *Homb. et Jacq., Voy. au Pole Sud., Zool.*, Vol. V., p. 10, 1854. Pl. IV. Fig. 24—27.

Shell umbilicated, depressed, rather solid, rather shining, closely, regularly, and rather strongly striately ribbed, either white and rather glossy, or pale horny ; spire slightly prominent, suture rather impressed ; whorls 5, slightly convex, the last convex and rather tumid, scarcely descending in front ; base with ribs smoother than above, umbilicus moderate, deep ; aperture lunately-ovate, slightly broader than high ; peristome thin, expanded, white within, margins approximating, columellar margin scarcely expanded above, and slightly reflected.
Diameter, greatest 0·70 ; *least* 0·57 ; *height* 0·35 *of an inch.*
Habitat. Islands of Torres Strait, from Nogo Island on the south to Warrior Island on the north.—*MacGillivray.*
A fine series of specimens has satisfied me regarding the correctness of the synonyms given above.

154. Helix Alexandræ. *Cox.* Plate VI. Fig. 1, *natural size and magnified.* M.C.
Cox, Catalogue of Australian Land Shells, p. 35, 1864.
Shell umbilicated, depressed, glassy, translucent, shining, faintly and

not regularly, finely, membranously ribbed; spire slightly prominent, suture impressed; whorls 4, regularly increasing, convex, last slightly deflected in front; base striated as above to the bottom of the perspective umbilicus, which equals $\frac{1}{4}$ of the diameter; aperture diagonal, nearly circular; peristome thickened, expanded, slightly reflected, white, margins nearly continuous.

Diameter, greatest 0·09; *least* 0·07; *height* 0·05 *of an inch.*
Habitat. Petersham. Marrickville. Glebe. Craigend, and other places about Sydney.—*Cox.*

A very neat little shell, of a delicate white, tinged with blue, and very closely allied to the European *H. costata* of Müller.

XXVI.—SECTION THERSITES. *Pfr.* Vers. p. 141.

* H. Richmondiana.   * H. Bidwilli.
* H. MacGillivrayi.   * H. delta.

155. Helix Richmondiana. *Pfr.* Plate VIII. Figs. 5 and 6.
Pfr., Pro. Zool. Soc., 1851, p. 252.
Reeve, Conc. Icon. sp. 365.

Shell imperforate, broadly trochiform, solid, opaque, shining, closely and irregularly, obliquely, finely striated and granulated, dark chestnut, reddish at the apex; spire conical, rounded at the apex; whorls 6, flattened, very gradually increasing, last slightly descending in front, sharply keeled at the periphery; base flat, aperture very oblique, triangularly ovate, at the keel pointedly produced in front, within glossy livid; peristome thickened, chestnut or blackish-brown, margins not approaching, joined with a thin callus, expanded and slightly reflected, especially towards the columella.

Diameter, greatest 2·20; *least* 2·00; *height* 1·00 *of an inch.*
Habitat. Richmond River, N. S. W.—*Cox.*

Apparently confined to that district, where it occurs in plenty along with *H. Falconari*, in the vast Cedar and Pine brushes, both keeping under logs, &c., in dry weather. A pale variety of this fine species is not uncommon, Fig. 6. The colour is reddish or yellowish, of various degrees of intensity, with a narrow, dark, spiral band, and a dark blotch in the umbilical region.

156. Helix MacGillivrayi. *Forbes.* Plate II. Fig. 12. M.C.
Forbes, Voy. of Rattlesnake, Vol. II., p. 377. Pl. III. Fig. 1.
Reeve, Conc. Icon. sp. 357.

Shell imperforate, trochiform, rather thin, smooth, moderately shining, very closely obliquely and spirally striated throughout, flesh coloured, irregularly interspersed with minute dark, rounded dots; spire conical, apex acute, bluish-black; whorls 5, flat, the last keeled, suddenly descending in front, beneath the keel somewhat compressed and convex; mouth very oblique, sinuately and irregularly triangular; peristome thin, white within, surrounded by a dark band, right margin arched, then forming a rounded projection, followed by a rounded sinus, thence to the columella slightly curved, columella slightly ascending, callous, dark chestnut at the base.

Diameter, greatest 0·90; *least* 0·75; *height* 0·67 *of an inch.*

Habitat. Frankland Isles, N. E. Coast of Australia, on trees.—*MacGillivray*.

A handsome and very singular shell, of which Forbes remarks that it strikingly resembles in shape some marine *Zizyphini*.

157. Helix Bidwilli. *Pfr.* Plate II. Fig. 3. M.C.
Pfr., Pro. Zool. Soc., 1853.
Reeve, Conc. Icon. sp. 1034.

Shell imperforate, pyramidally-conical, smooth, very faintly obliquely striatulated, shining, white, marked with small burnt red spots, for the most part arranged spirally, and largest about the mouth; spire regularly conical, suture very slightly impressed; whorls 6, very nearly flat, last carinated, slightly swollen in front, and constricted at the mouth; base flat, with larger and darker blotches than above; aperture very oblique, somewhat oval; peristome black, thinly rounded, slightly reflected on the left, margins not approximating, but joined by a very thin dark callus.

Diameter, greatest 0·70; *least* 0·63; *height* 0·65 *of an inch.*
Habitat. Mary River and Ipswich, Queensland.—*Bidwell*. Richmond River, N. S. W.—*MacGillivray*.

A handsome trochiform shell, which ascends smooth-stemmed trees in the brushes to the height of 30 feet and upwards. It was originally found by the late Mr. Bidwill, C.C.L.

158. Helix delta. *Pfr.* Plate IV. Fig. 13, *natural size and magnified.* M.C.
Pfr., Pro. Zool. Soc., 1856, p. 386.
Helix conoidea. *Cox, Catalogue of Australian Land Shells*, p. 21, 1864.
Helix fenestrata. *Cox, Pro. Zool. Soc.*, 1866, p. 374.

Shell perforated, globosely-conical, keeled, thin, fleshy white, with numerous faintly irregular elevated ribs, under the lens shewing more minute spiral decussating lines, giving a fenestrated appearance to the shell, especially towards the apex; spire conical, obtuse; whorls 6, slightly convex, last somewhat sharply keeled; aperture diagonal, sub-angularly-lunate, pearly within; peristome simple, thin, acute, very slightly expanded on the columella above and reflected, somewhat covering the minute umbilicus.

Diameter, greatest 0·40; *least* 0·35; *height* 0·25 *of an inch.*
Habitat. Drayton Range, Queensland.—*Stutchbury*. Cabbage Tree Island, Port Stephens, N. S. W.—*King*. Pine Mountain, Lismore, Richmond River, N. S. W., on trunks of trees.—*MacGillivray*.

The fenestration of this very distinct, carinated, and widely conical shell is sometimes indistinct.

XXVII.—SECTION TACHEA. *Pfr.* Vers. p. 142.

* H. tescorum. * H. Dringi.

159. Helix tescorum. *Bens.* Plate IX. Fig. 5, *copied from Reeve.*
Reeve, Con. Icon. sp. 1154.
Benson, *Ann. and Mag., Nat. Hist.*, 1853, p. 30.

Shell imperforate, conoidly-globose, solid, whitish (an colorata?),

(greenish horny, *Reeve*), irregularly striated; spire conoid, rather obtuse, suture deeply channelled; whorls 5½, slightly convex, last rounded, deflected in front; aperture diagonal, roundly-lunate; peristome thickened, right margin scarcely expanded, basal reflected, columellar margin dilated, appressed (columellar margin reflected, broadly callously dilated over the umbilical area, *Reeve*).
Diameter, greatest 0·77; *least* 0·68; *height* 0·41 *of an inch.*
Habitat. Shark's Bay, Western Australia.—*Benson.*

Pfeiffer's description is that given above from *Mon. Hel. Viv.*, Vol. IV., p. 233. Benson states that it was found along with *H. plectilis*, and appeared to be in a *sub-fossil* state.

Reeve remarks that this species "has a worn opaque-white aspect, but it has some faint traces of rusty-brown, so that the species in fine condition may probably be coloured."

160. Helix Dringi. *Pfr.* Plate XI. Fig. 9, *copied from Reeve.*
Pfr., Symbolæ, Vol. III., p. 73.
Reeve, Conc. Icon. sp. 769.

Shell with a covered umbilicus, depressed, thin, fragile, above very closely and very finely plicated, whitish, opaque, girt with pellucid lines; spire somewhat flattened; whorls 4½, scarcely convex, last slightly compressed on the side, smooth at the base, inflated; aperture lunar, of one colour; peristome expanded, somewhat thickened within, columellar margin shortly arched, dilated, reflected, and appressed.
Diameter, greatest 0·51; *least* 0·43; *height* 0·29 *of an inch.*
Habitat. Eastern Australia, near Torres Strait, under decayed leaves. —*Dring.*

I have given Pfeiffer's description. The specimen is unique. Reeve speaks of it as a delicate flatly, globose, opaque, white species, encircled with pellucid bands and lines.

XXVIII.—SECTION CALLICOCHLIAS. *Pfr.* Vers. p. 143.

* H. Fraseri. * H. Mitchellæ.

161. Helix Fraseri. *Gray.* Plate X. Fig. 6. M.C.
Gray, Pro. Zool. Soc., 1836, p. 63, and in *Griffith's Anim. Kingd. Moll.* Pl. XXXVI.
Reeve, Conc. Icon. sp. 360.

Shell imperforate, globosely-turbinated, smooth, very faintly obliquely striated, under the lens exhibiting extremely minute spiral lines and lengthened granulations not perceptible to the touch, reddish-yellow, with numerous spiral chestnut lines and bands, darker about the mouth; spire broadly conical, obtuse; whorls 6, slightly convex, last convex, above deflected in front; base marked as above, but granulations more distinct; aperture diagonal, ovately-lunate, black within, then of a shining livid hue; peristome straight, broadly expanded, reflected, margins rather approaching, and connected by

a very thin callus, columellar margin much thickened above and expanded.
Diameter, greatest 2·00 ; *least* 1·60 ; *height* 1·10 *of an inch.*
Habitat. Clarence and Richmond Rivers, N. S. W. Brisbane and Wide Bay, Queensland.
A variable shell. The preceding description applies to what I consider to be the typical form, with black lip and decided markings. A larger variety, of which one individual measures 2·25 ; 1·75 ; 1·70 *of an inch*, is scarcely so brightly marked, and has the lip and columella of an obscure violaceous or livid hue. Reeve's figure and Pfeiffer's description, *Mon. Hel. Viv.*, Vol. I., p. 246, apply more particularly to this variety. A very beautiful variety from the Clarence River, smooth and glossy, the sculpture being reduced to its minimum, is of an intense blackish-chestnut, gradually fading into pale reddish-chestnut at the apex. Another variety, although dark and unbanded below, has the spire pale, and finely spirally lined; and there are several others.

162. Helix Mitchellæ. *Cox.* Plate IX. Fig. 9. M C.
Cox, Catalogue of Australian Land Shells, p. 19, 1864.
Shell imperforate, globosely-turbinated, solid, striated with the lines of growth, under the lens universally reticularly or irregularly linearly granulated, deep reddish-chestnut, with four yellow bands, one broad in umbilical region, another narrow along the periphery, with a blackish band above it, a third, broader and separated by a dark band from a very narrow fourth at the suture; spire roundly convex, obtuse; whorls $6\frac{1}{2}$, very regularly increasing, convex, last deflected in front, convex below ; aperture very oblique, truncately-elliptical, within of a pearly bluish tint; peristome thickened, lipped within, reflected, inner edge glossy, chestnut black, margins connected with a thin dark callus, anterior rather sinuated near the periphery, columellar margin flattened, with a very prominent inner lip, having an obsolete tooth-like callosity near the centre.
Diameter, greatest 1·80 ; *least* 1·50 ; *height* 1·20 *of an inch.*
Habitat. Clarence River, N. S. W.—*Mitchell.* Beach Hut, Emmigrant Creek, Richmond River, under masses of dead leaves.—*Cox.*
This fine species, the specimen of which described and figured, is from the cabinet of Mrs. Mitchell; but I have received since several fine specimens from the locality above mentioned. It is extremely interesting, from its wonderful resemblance in sculpture and coloration to *H. Dupuyana*, a depressly-conical and carinated species. We see here how, in two groups, or sections of the great genus *Helix*, one in each beautifully represents the other.

XXIX.—SECTION GEOTROCHUS. *Pfr.* Vers. p. 145.

* H. Dupuyana.   * H. fucata.   * H. Gärtneriana.
* H. consecndens.   * H. Poiretiana.   * H. Novæ-Hollandiæ.

163. Helix Dupuyana. *Pfr.* Plate II. Fig. 5. M.C.
Pfr., Pro. Zool. Soc., 1851, p. 159.
Reeve, Conc. Icon. sp. 354.

Shell imperforate, depressly-conical, solid, the lines of growth sometimes rather diagonally decussated, prominent and rugose, with very faint lines, and the whole surface has a minutely granularly reticulated appearance under the lens, rich chestnut, with two narrow fulvous bands, one below the suture, the other on the periphery, and the latter with a faint dark band above it; spire broadly conoid, obtuse at the apex; whorls 5½, flatly convex, last deflected in front, angled at the periphery, swollen at the mouth, and rather excavated above; base usually with a yellowish mark round the umbilical region; aperture very oblique, truncately oval; peristome thickened, lipped within, slightly expanded, callous, very dark glossy-chestnut, as is the thin callus connecting the margins and the base of the columella, on which, at the centre, is a long tooth-like callosity.

Diameter, greatest 1·45; *least* 1·20; *height* 0·80 *of an inch*.

Habitat. Ash Island and Hexham, Hunter River.—*Scott*. Bellinger and Upper Clarence Rivers, N. S W.—*Cox*.

Rather a variable species, as may be seen by comparing the figures and descriptions quoted above. Pfeiffer, *Mon. Hel. Viv.*, Vol. IV., p. 200, mentions what he calls var. β. as being more depressed, with a convexly-conoid spire, chestnut, with one yellow band at the periphery, and another in the umbilical region. Add a second yellow band under the suture, and one has the type and commonest form as described above.

164. Helix Gärtneriana. *Pfr.* Plate XI. Fig 11, *copied from Reeve.*

Pfr., *Pro. Zool. Soc.*, 1851, p. 255.
Reeve, *Conc. Icon.* sp. 419.

Shell umbilicated, cone-shaped, solid, irregularly elevatedly striated, opaque, slightly shining, yellowish-flesh coloured; spire conical, apex obtuse; suture somewhat margined; whorls 7, convex, last sub-angular at the periphery, encircled by a red line, not descending in front, beneath rather flat; umbilicus very narrow, open; aperture slightly oblique, somewhat square; peristome white, upper margin almost angularly arched, expanded, basal nearly straight, columellar margin pinkish, short, vertical and reflected.

Diameter, greatest 0·87; *least* 0·75; *height* 0·87 *of an inch*.

Habitat. Port Essington.—*MacGillivray.*

The preceding description has been taken verbatim, except the locality, from Pfeiffer's *Mon. Hel. Viv.*, Vol. III., p. 220. Reeve remarks that the columellar margin is stained with a characteristic purple violet blotch.

165. Helix Poiretiana. *Pfr.* Plate II. Fig. 1. M.C.

Pfr., *Pro. Zool. Soc.*, 1851, p. 254.
Reeve, *Conc. Icon.* sp. 418.

Shell perforate, conical, rather solid, smooth, rather shining, opaque, very finely obliquely striated, fleshy white, frequently irregularly streaked with pale brown along the lines of growth; spire very tall, conical, suture impressed; whorls 7, nearly flat, last more rounded, convex below, with a narrow reddish-brown band under the pheriphery, very slightly descending in front; aperture diagonal, lunately rounded; peristome expanded, reflected, thin edged, margins not approaching, columellar margin thicker and nearly concealing the narrow umbilicus.

Diameter, greatest 0·80; *least* 0·70; *height* 1·00 *of an inch.*

Habitat. Night Island, N. E. Coast of Australia, on trees.—*MacGillivray* and *Edwards.*

Several mistakes regarding identity and locality between this and *H. Güertneriana* have been made by Pfeiffer, Forbes, Reeve, and myself. This shell, I am enabled to state with certainty, is not from Port Essington as originally stated. It was first found in the locality indicated by me during the voyage of the Beagle, and subsequently during that of the Rattlesnake, and since then it has twice been collected there for me in abundance. It is curious that this fine shell should apparently be completely confined to one little island, the dry portion of which is not more than a quarter of a mile in length.

166. Helix fucata. *Pfr.* Plate II. Fig. 8. M.C.
Pfr., Pro. Zool. Soc., 1853, p. 59.
Reeve, Conc. Icon. sp. 1029.

Shell imperforate, globosely-conical, rather solid, shining, porcellaneous, under the lens obliquely striated, also but more faintly, spirally and decussatedly striated, white, with three black spiral bands, and another faint reddish one above each of the central bands; spire sharply conical, acute and reddish at the apex, suture smooth; whorls 5, nearly flat, last convex, scarcely descending; base rather flat, with a black umbilical mark; aperture diagonal, lunately-oval; peristome thin, right margin rather straight, anterior produced and curved, left expanded and reflected, collumellar margin tinged with pink.

Diameter, greatest 0·65; *least* 0·55; *height* 0·50 *of an inch.*

Habitat. Wide Bay and Maryborough, Queensland.—*Strange* and *Bidwill.*

A very beautifully painted glossy shell, resembling a South Sea Island group, illustrated by *H. Boivini.*

167. Helix conscendens. *Cox.* Plate II. Fig. 6. M.C.
Cox, Pro. Zool. Soc., 1866, p. 374.

Shell imperforate, globosely conical, very thin, pellucid, somewhat glassy, rather shining, under the lens obsoletely obliquely striated, whitish, with one band more or less conspicuously coloured; spire conical, coloured at the tip; whorls 6, slightly convex, last very large, slightly deflected, with an obsolete keel; aperture diagonal, lunately-ovate; peristome thin, outer margin somewhat sinuated, columella above slightly reflected.

Diameter, greatest 0·60; *least* 0·50; *height* 0·55 *of an inch.*

Habitat. Lismore, Upper Richmond River, on trees in the pine brushes.—*MacGillivray.*

The band varies in intensity of colour, from deep black bordered with red to reddish-brown or pinkish, and in old specimens is very faintly indicated. This species is closely related to the many banded and lined *H. fucata* of Wide Bay.

168. Helix Novæ-Hollandiæ. *Gray.*
Carocolla Novæ-Hollandiæ. *Gray, Pro. Zool. Soc.*, 1834, p. 67.
Shell orbicular, conical, sub-depressed, sub-perforate, thin, smooth, very finely elevately-punctate, pale fulvous; spire conical, convex; whorls 6, distinct, with a brown sub-median band, last with a pale angular keel, convex in front, deep brown about the axis; aperture sub-angular; peristome sub-inflexed behind the keel, somewhat thickened, reflected, black, outer lip thin, brown, throat whitish, with a pellucid band.
Diameter 14 *lines, axis* 9 *lines.*
Habitat. N. S. W. 200 miles from Port Macquarie.—*Cunningham.*
This description is a translation of the original. After much reflection I feel scarcely any doubt of the specific identity of this shell with *H. Dupuyana*, a point which inspection of the original specimen will probably settle at once in the affirmative, and if so, Dr. Gray's name has the priority.

Genus
BULIMUS.—Scopoli.

Shell oblong or turreted; aperture with unequal longitudinal margins, toothless or dentate; columella entire, revolute externally or nearly simple; peristome simple or expanded.

Animal like Helix.—*Woodward*, p. 164.

XXX.—SECTION NAPÆUS. *Pfr.* Vers. p. 153.
* B. Pacificus. *Pfr.* * B. lepidula. *Ad. and Ang.*
* B. Adelaidæ. *Ad. and Ang.*

169. Bulimus Pacificus. *Pfr.* Plate XIII. Fig. 3. M.C.
Pfr., Mon. Hel. Viv., Vol. IV., p. 414.
Pupa Pacifica. *Pfr., Pro. Zool Soc.*, p. 31, 1846.
Shell deeply fissured, ovately-cylindrical, very finely obliquely striated, rather solid, yellowish-horny; apex rounded; whorls 5, convex, last nearly equalling ½ of the entire length; aperture lunately-rounded or semi-oval; peristome white, lipped, shortly expanded, right lip briefly curved above with generally a small callous tubercle close to it on the body whorl, then nearly straight, rounded in front, columellar margin more expanded.

Length 0·15 ; breadth 0·10 ; aperture 0·05 long, of an inch.
Habitat. Brisbane, Ipswich, Port Curtis, &c., along the coasts and islands of Queensland, to Cape York and the islands of Torres Strait.—*MacGillivray.*

170. Bulimus lepidula. *Ad. and Ang.*
Bulimulus (Chondrula) lepidula. *Adams and Angas, Pro. Zool. Soc.,* p. 38, 1864.

Shell turreted, pupiform, umbilicated, thin, shining, semi-pellucid, horny ; whorls 5, strongly convex, longitudinally striated ; aperture roundly-ovate ; peristome interrupted, white, widely reflected ; mouth above with a small, white, tubercular callosity.

Length 2 lines ; breadth 1 line.

Habitat. Shark's Bay, N. W. Australia.—*Angas.*

It is remarked by the authors quoted above, whose description I have given unaltered, that this little species differs from *B. Adelaidæ,* in being semi-pellucid, shining, and of a horn colour, also that the whorls are much more strongly convex.

171. Bulimus Adelaidæ. *Ad. and Ang.* M.C.
Buliminus (Chondrula) Adelaidæ. *Adams and Angas, Pro. Zool. Soc.,* p. 522, 1863.
Pupa Ramsayi. *Cox, Catalogue of Australian Land Shells,* p. 28, 1864.

Shell umbilicated, somewhat fusiformly cylindrical, rather solid, very finely longitudinally striated, pale brown, or whitish ; whorls 6, rather convex, apex rounded, four first gradually increasing, 5th and 6th of equal width, last equalling about ¼ of the length ; aperture vertical, oval obliquely truncated ; peristome white, expanded, right margin curved, with a conspicuous white tooth-like callosity in the angle, columellar margin much more callous and expanded.

Length 0·24 ; breadth 0·10 ; aperture 0·06 long, of an inch.

Habitat. Probably generally distributed in South Australia. My specimens are from Rapid Bay, and Wallaroo.—*Masters.*

XXXI.—SECTION OPEAS. *Pfr.* VERS. p. 156.

* B. Tuckeri.

172. Bulimus Tuckeri. *Pfr.* Plate XIII. Fig. 9. M.C.
Pfr., Pro. Zool. Soc., 1846, p. 30.
Reeve, Conc. Icon. sp. 481.
Bulimus Walli. *Cox, Catalogue of Australian Land Shells,* p. 24, 1864.

Shell perforate, cylindrically acuminate, very thin, shining, distinctly longitudinally striated, glassy, whitish or pale yellowish ; spire very long, tapering, obtuse at the apex ; whorls 8, convex, last equalling ¼ of the entire length ; aperture of a long oval form ; peristome simple, acute, columellar margin nearly straight, very slightly dilated above.

Length 0·42 ; breadth 0·10 ; aperture 0·10 long, of an inch.

Habitat. Clarence Heads, N. S. W. Generally distributed throughout Queensland and its islands, from Brisbane to Cape York. Found generally in the isles of the S. W. Pacific, and has been introduced to Sydney with plants from Aneiteum.—*MacGillivray*.

Varies considerably in size, and slightly in acuteness of the spire, and also in the distinctness of the longitudinal striæ.

The specimens formerly described by me as *B. Walli*, I can now only look upon as a variety of this species of exaggerated length.

XXXII.—SECTION CARYODES. *Pfr.* Vers. p. 157.

* B. Dufresni. * B. Angasianus.

173. Bulimus Dufresni. *Leach.* Plate XIII. Fig. 12. M.C.
Leach, *Miscell. Zool.*, p. 153. Pl. CXX.
Helix Dufresni. *Fer., Hist.* Pl. CXIII. Fig. 1—3.

Shell imperforate, ovately-oblong, rather solid, shining, and almost smooth, although faintly marked with longitudinal striæ and granulations, chestnut brown, encircled by yellow and blackish bands; spire obtuse, suture crenulated below; whorls 5, slightly convex, last nearly equalling the spire; aperture oval, very slightly oblique, bluish within; peristome simple, rounded on the edge, frequently moderately thickened, right and basal margins regularly and moderately arcuate, columellar margin partially twisted in the centre, and above slightly expanded and adherent.

Length 1·60; breadth 0·80; *aperture* 0·80 *long*; 0·50 *wide, of an inch*.

Habitat. Tasmania. Widely distributed and very abundant.—*Cox*.

A handsome and variable species. One median spiral band is generally present, usually flanked with two paler ones. Sometimes there are longitudinal markings in addition. Some stunted varieties do not exceed 8-10ths of an inch in length.

174. Bulimus Angasianus. *Pfr.* Plate XIII. Fig. 2. M.C.
Pfr., Pro. Zool. Soc., p. 528, 1863.

Shell imperforate, rather broadly and conically ovate, thin, translucent, shining, very closely and smoothly striately ribbed, the striæ very conspicuous at the sutures, decussated with spiral lines, especially above, pale horny, reddish-brown, with two bright yellow bands generally margined with brown lines; spire short, conical, obtuse, apex granular; whorls 4, convex, last longer than the spire, rounded at the base; aperture angularly oval, within pearly, and showing the two bands white instead of yellow; peristome simple, regular, thin, columellar margin whitely callous, slightly expanded, and outwardly reflected, but sometimes leaving a fissure leading to the covered umbilicus.

Length 0·90; breadth 0·50; *aperture* 0·50 *long*; 0·35 *broad, of an inch*.

Habitat. Port Lincoln, S. Australia, on an open heath.—*Angas*.

Among the numerous specimens collected by Mr. Masters of this species a striking variety occurs. It is of a beautiful bright yellow colour, with indications of a single reddish spiral line.

XXXIII.—SECTION LIPARUS. *Pfr.* Vers. p. 157.

* B. atomatus.

175. Bulimus atomatus. *Gray.* Plate XIII. Fig. 8; and Plate XVIII. Fig. 15. M.C.
Gray, Pro. Zool. Soc., 1834, p. 64.
Reeve, Conc. Icon. sp. 184.

Shell imperforate, acutely ovate, thin, translucent, slightly shining, thickly marked with flattened longitudinal striæ, decussated with irregular spiral lines, pale yellowish-brown, thickly covered with dark markings, mostly in interrupted streaks, spots, and zigzag lines; spire conical, rather blunt at the apex; whorls 5, moderately convex, last equalling about 4-7th of the entire length; aperture narrowly oval, bluish within; peristome simple, straight, thin, outer and anterior margins regularly arched, columellar margin nearly straight, and vertical above, slightly expanded and reflected, quite covering the umbilicus, and leaving only a small shallow groove in its place.

Length 2·30; *breadth* 1·25; *aperture* 1·10 *long*; 0·65 *wide, of an inch.*

Habitat. 70 miles from Port Macquarie.—*Cunningham.* Ash Island and Hexham, Hunter River.—*Scott.* Port Stephens. Manning River, N. S. W.—*King.*

This seems a fit place to mention, as this description is somewhat at variance with Pfeiffer's, that the number of whorls, one less than he makes it, is counted from a front view, and as is also the proportion between the last whorl and the rest of the shell, which is simply the relation of the mouth. He gives no directions on these points, as he does regarding measurements.

XXXIV.—SECTION MESEMBRINUS. *Pfr.* Vers. p. 158.

* B. dux. * B. inflatus. * B. Tasmanicus.

176. Bulimus dux. *Pfr.* Plate XIII. Fig. 4; and Plate XVIII. Fig. 16. M.C.
Pfr., Pro. Zool. Soc., p. 24, 1861.

Shell sub-perforate, elongately-oval, solid, opaque, not shining, with numerous longitudinal and irregular, generally flattened, lines of growth, decussated more or less distinctly above with spiral lines, dull greyish-white; spire short, conical, acute at the apex, suture slightly impressed, crenulated, margined; whorls 5 to 5½, very slightly convex, last rather more than half the entire length; aperture narrowly oval, rosy-pink within; peristome simple, straight; columella dilated and reflected, almost entirely concealing the umbilical fissure.

Length 1·90; *breadth* 1·10; *aperture* 1·05 *long*; 0·50 *broad, of an inch.*
Habitat. King George's Sound, W. Australia.—*Masters.*

A very remarkable, large, solid, whitish shell, resembling a semi-fossil.

177. Bulimus inflatus. *Lam.* Plate XII. Fig. 14, *copied from Reeve.*
Lamarck, Anim. sans Vertebr., Edt. Deshayes., Vol. VIII., p. 230.
Reeve, Conc. Icon. sp. 512.

Shell perforate, ovate, ventricose, longitudinally roughly striated, solid, dead white; spire conical, blunt; whorls 5 to 5½, rather convex, last scarcely exceeding the spire; aperture oval; peristome simple, acute, columellar margin rather broadly dilated and reflected, not concealing the umbilicus.

Length 0·75; *breadth* 0·43; *aperture* 0·41 *long*; 0·21 *broad, of an inch.*
Habitat. New Holland.—*Deshayes.*

Never having seen this shell, which may be looked upon as doubtfully Australian, I have compiled the above from Pfeiffer's *Mon. Hel. Viv.*, Vol. II., p. 189, having also Reeve's description and plate before me. A very large specimen is stated to measure 1·06 *by* 0·55 *of an inch.*

178. Bulimus Tasmanicus. *Pfr.* Plate XIII. Fig. 1.
Pfr., Pro. Zool. Soc., p. 260, 1851.

Shell imperforate, conically-ovate, rather solid, translucent, with little lustre, flatly and rather coarsely longitudinally striated, whitish, originally covered with a reddish-brown epidermis, often remaining as long close streaks along the lines of growth, but frequently entirely absent when the surface may have a dull chalky appearance; spire reddish, and papillary at the apex; whorls 5, slightly convex, last nearly thrice the length of the spire, rounded at the base; aperture very slightly oblique, of a rather lengthened oval, pale yellow within; peristome simple, straight, thin, columellar margin very slightly rolled back.

Length 1·10; *breadth* 0·60; *aperture* 0·65 *long*; 0·40 *broad, of an inch.*
Habitat. Tasmania, climbing on trees.—*Gunn.*

A shell varying in relative length and breadth, but more so in markings, from the absence or presence of the coloured epidermis.

XXXV.—SECTION RHABDOTUS. *Pfr.* Vers. p. 158.

* B. Bidwilli   * B. Baconi.   * B. indutus.
* B. bulla.   * B. Onslowi.   * B. melo.
* B. Kingi.   * B. rhodostoma.   * B. Mastersi.

179. Bulimus Bidwilli. *Cox.* Plate XIII. Fig. 11. Museum, Rev. R. L. King.

Shell nearly imperforate, of a lengthened oval form, rather thin, smooth, very indistinctly striated, not shining, white, with numerous black and reddish spiral bands, and, on each whorl, more or less distinctly, a band of elongated black or reddish markings; spire acutely conical, bluish at the tip; whorls 6, very slightly convex, last not ventricose, deeply and irregularly stained with black and red; aperture uprightly oval; peristome simple, regular, thin, columellar margin

white, slightly expanded and reflected, but not quite covering the umbilical orifice.
Length 0·77; breadth 0·40; aperture 0·40 long; 0·30 broad, of an inch.
Habitat. Burnett River, Queensland, on the tops of trees.—*Bidwill*.
The only gaily painted Australian *Bulimus* known. Notwithstanding habit, mode of colouration, and geographical remoteness, it ought, I think, to come next to *B. Kingi*.

180. Bulimus Baconi. *Benson*.
Benson, Ann. and Mag. of Nat. Hist., Vol. XIII., p. 99, 1854.
Shell perforate, ovate, thin, closely striated, the upper portion of the whorls somewhat granulated from spiral striæ, silky, pellucid, yellowish, with two chestnut bands; spire very slightly convexly-conical, apex obtuse, papillary; whorls 5, slightly convex, crenulated at the suture, last inflated, scarcely exceeding the spire in length; aperture hardly oblique, oval, within coloured as without, but paler; peristome simple, straight, right margin above somewhat spreading and turned up, columellar margin brownish violet, above dilated and reflected.
Length 0·94; breadth 1·55; aperture 0·53 long; 0·31 broad, of an inch.
Habitat. Darling Range, W. Australia.—*Bacon*.
The preceding description has been taken, verbatim, from that of Pfeiffer, in *Mon. Hel. Viv.*, Vol. IV., p. 479. Benson remarks that in its transverse bands and colouring this shell differs from all the W. Australian species, and inclines to the Tasmanian *B. Dufresni*.

181. Bulimus indutus. *Menke*. Plate XIII. Fig. 10.
Menke, Moll. Nov. Holl. Spec., p. 6, 1843.
Shell perforate, oblong and acutely ovate, solid, rather shining, longitudinally striated, and under the lens rugose above, white under a reddish-yellow epidermis; spire obtuse at the apex, suture crenulated; whorls 5, very slightly convex, last equalling the spire; aperture elliptically-ovate, white within; peristome simple, acute; columella thickened above and slightly dilated, whitish or flesh coloured.
Length 1·50; breadth 0·70; aperture 0·75 long; 0·50 broad, of an inch.
Habitat. Darling Range and Mount Eliza, W. Australia.—*Priess*. Perth, W. Australia.—*Bacon*.
In my collection there are two specimens of a shell from Mr. Cuming, marked "*B. rhodostoma*," Western Australia. As these agree with the original description of *B. indutus* of Menke, and that of Pfeiffer, *Mon. Hel. Viv.*, I have made out the above description by collating from all three sources. At the same time it appears to me highly probable that the two are specifically identical; the markings, and colour of the mouth within, are not good points of difference, unless confirmed by others, and Gray's name has the priority.

182. Bulimus bulla. *Menke*.
Menke, Moll. Nov. Holl. Spec., p. 7, 1843.
Shell perforate, elliptically-ovate, rather solid, longitudinally striated, white under a thin greenish-yellow epidermis, with brown ribbons

and bands; whorls 6, convex above, somewhat margined and fringed at the suture; spire moderate, obtuse; aperture elliptically-ovate, throat white; columella straight, lip acute.

Habitat. Darling Range, W. Australia.—*Priess.* Perth, W. Australia.—*Bacon.*

There are two varieties: *A.* with a band at the base and beneath the suture, and continuous brown somewhat bundled scattered ribbons—*length* 10, *breadth* 6 *lines*. *B.* with a single band beneath the suture, and two other obsolete interrupted brown bands in the middle of the last whorl.

The description is a mere translation of the original as quoted above, for I have never seen a specimen.

183. Bulimus Onslowi. *Cox.* Plate XIII. Fig. 13. Australian Museum.

Cox, *Catalogue of Australian Land Shells*, p. 24, 1864.

Shell perforate, broadly ovate, rather solid, somewhat shining, striated, surrounded by spiral decussating lines, giving the surface a rough granular appearance on the upper half, whitish, with numerous deeply reddish longitudinal irregular bands and blotches; spire very short, broadly conical, obtuse, suture crenulated; whorls 4, rather convex, last much inflated, longer than the spire; aperture elliptically-ovate, reddish-brown, and cloudy within; peristome simple, acute, columellar margin white, expanded and reflected, covering and nearly concealing the narrow perforation.

Length 0·80; *breadth* 0·55; *aperture* 0·55 *long*; 0·30 *broad, of an inch*.

Habitat. Dirk Hartog's Island, W. Australia.—*Capt. Onslow.*

A very distinct, remarkably inflated, and shortly spired species, beautifully striped with red and white.

184. Bulimus melo. *Quoy et Gaimard.* Plate XIII. Fig. 6. M.C.

Helix melo. *Quoy et Gaimard, Voy. d' Astr., Zool.*, Vol. II., p. 109. Pl. IX. Fig. 4—5.

Helix melo. Var. *Quoy et Gaimard, Voy. d' Astr., Zool.*, Vol. II., p. 110. Plate IX. Fig. 6—7.

Bulimus melo. *Reeve, Conc. Icon.* sp. 243.

Bulimus physoides. *Reeve, Conc. Icon.* sp. 507.

Shell perforate, ovate, solid, rather shining, longitudinally rugosely striated, seldom strongly, except under the sutures, whitish or pale yellow, with or without irregular reddish or chestnut streaks, and a red sutural band; spire conical, rather acute; whorls 5, slightly convex, last swollen, rather less than equalling or exceeding the spire; aperture oval; peristome simple, straight, acute, gradually roundly merging into the columellar margin, which is rather callous, expanded, and reflected, nearly covering the narrow but always open umbilical fissure.

Length 1·20; *breadth* 0·70; *aperture* 0·70 *long*; 0·40 *wide, of an inch*.

Habitat. King George's Sound.—*Quoy et Gaimard. Masters, &c.* District Hay, W. Australia, on a species of melaleuca, gregarious in October.—*Priess, apud Menke.* Freemantle, W. Australia.—*Bacon.*

This species, which far exceeds *B. Kingi* in diversity of markings, conspicuously differs from it in the first instance by its greater solidity and less lengthened form. Menke, *Moll. Nov. Holl. Spec.*, p. 7, 1843, specifies four varieties. Pfeiffer gives descriptions of six, *Mon. Hel. Viv.*, Vol. IV., p. 477; and my own collection could furnish others. Yet a few are pretty constant in their characters. The description given above applies to what is perhaps the most usual, the pale coloured type. These pale shells have almost a porcellaneous appearance; they may be entirely unmarked, have a sutural band of reddish-chestnut, with or without longitudinal streaks of the same, pale and indistinct, or numerous and deeply coloured, &c.; the mouth within is white, or shewing a pinkish hue, and there is very frequently a fleshy tint on the columella and about the umbilicus.

Of the dark series, the most remarkable, which includes my largest specimens, are very closely and narrowly longitudinally streaked, with white, chestnut, or reddish-brown, &c. The interior of the mouth is purplish, darker in proportion to the colour of the shell. In old specimens the columella is very much thickened and callous above, but the umbilicus is never completely closed. This last is Pfeiffer's var. δ., and is represented by Reeve, sp. 213. A much smaller dark variety, nearly black, with a reddish apex, and very finely longitudinally streaked with white threads, has a single reddish spiral band, and the mouth is black within.

A variety found along with the preceding by Mr. Masters, on an island in King George's Sound, has a very pale chestnut ground, a reddish apex, a dark spiral band under the suture, and is handsomely streaked with dark chestnut and threads of white. Lastly, there is one prominently streaked blackish and reddish, which has three markings, interrupted by light spiral bands.

185. Bulimus Kingi. *Gray.* Plate XIII. Fig. 7. M.C.
Gray, *Ann of Phil.*, *New Ser.*, Vol. IX., p. 414, 1825.
Reeve, *Conc. Icon.* sp. 336.
Helix trilineata. *Quoy et Gaimard, Voy. d'Astr., Zool.*, Vol. II., p. 107. Pl. IX. Fig. 1—3.
Ferussac et Deshaye's *Hist. Moll. Atlas*, Vol. II., 1832. Pl. CL. Fig. 11—12.
Bulimus trilineatus. *Reeve, Conc. Icon.* sp. 310, and sp. 397.
Bulimus Sayi. *Pfr., Pro Zool. Soc.*, 1846, p. 114.
Reeve, *Conc. Icon.* sp. 458.
Bulimus melo. Var. β., *Menke, Moll. Nov. Holl. Spec.*, p. 7, 1843.

Shell nearly imperforate, of a lengthened oval, rather solid, translucent, rather shining, closely, irregularly, and rather strongly striated, especially at the sutures, whitish, streaked longitudinally with very numerous, flame-like, interrupted or continuous dark chestnut markings; spire conical, rather acute; whorls 6, very slightly convex, last not ventricose, usually rather shorter than the spire, frequently equalling and rarely slightly exceeding it; aperture oval to oblong-oval, shining within, purplish-chestnut; peristome simple, acute; columella callously white, with a dark patch outside, slightly dilated and reflected, reducing the vestige of an umbilicus to a very slight aperture.

Length 1·15; *breadth*, 0·55; *aperture* 0·55 *long* ; 0·30 *broad, of an inch.*

Habitat. Bald Head, King George's Sound, W. Australia.—*King. Quoy and Gaimard*, and *Masters*.

A great deal of confusion has been unnecessarily created with reference to *B. Kingi* in its relationship to *B. trilineatus*. Nearly twenty years ago Pfeiffer, *Mon. Hel. Viv.*, Vol. II., p. 174, observed that *B. trilineatus* seemed to be a variety of *B. Kingi*. It would have been better perhaps had he acted upon this opinion, which might have saved three out of the four figures, with descriptions in Reeve, which are calculated to confound. Let the reader carefully compare the plates and descriptions of sp. 310, and sp. 397, and he will see a good example of attempted conchological mystification, without any excuse on the score of difficulty.

Having examined many hundred specimens of *Bulimi* other than *B. melo*, collected at King George's Sound by Mr. Masters, I feel no hesitation whatever in referring them to one species. Those corresponding with Gray's original description of *B. Kingi*, as being conically-ovate, with aperture equal to the spire and being inside the mouth of a purplish black, are easily picked out; but there exist gradations between such and the ovately-conical shape, with spire longer than the last whorl of *Quoy and Gaimard's* original description of *B. trilineatus*, I therefore join them. My description applies to shells exhibiting the most usual style of marking, including the short *Kingi* and the long *trilineata*, marked precisely alike, and in shape graduating as one series. Among the varieties one is whitish with very faint yellowish streaks; this has the mouth white within. Another pale variety, with more frequent, but very narrow dark streaks, has the darkened mouth and dark columella patch of the description. This is always a much thinner shell than *B. melo*, more elongated, and not inflated.

Here I take the liberty of referring to the figure in Wood's *Index Testaceologicus*, edition by Hanley, 1856—*Helix*. Plate VII. Fig. 27 a.—for the purpose of expressing my admiration of the ingenuity displayed in producing a figure so utterly at variance with what it is intended to represent; yet, the very next figure, that of *B. Dufresni*, although also on a very small scale, is remarkably good.

186. Bulimus rhodostoma. *Gray.* Plate XII. Fig 13, *copied from Reeve.*

Gray, *Pro. Zool. Soc.*, 1834, p. 65.
Reeve, *Conc. Icon.* sp. 323.

Shell narrowly umbilicated, ovate, solid, striated, obsoletely decussated above with concentric lines, reddish-yellow, clouded with rose colour, obsoletely banded with brown; spire conical, acute; whorls 7, scarcely convex, last scarcely exceeding the spire; suture somewhat crenulated; columella nearly straight; aperture ovately-oblong, rose coloured within; peristome simple, obtuse, margins sub-parallel, columellar margin reflected, vaulted.

Length 1·22; *breadth*, 0·67; *aperture* 0·69 *long*; 0·33 *broad, of an inch.*
Habitat. New Holland.—*Gray.*

187. Bulimus Mastersi. *Cox.* Plate XIII. Fig 14. M.C.
Cox, *Pro. Zool. Soc.*, 1867, p. 39.

Shell imperforate, ovately-conical, rather solid, rugosely-plicate, sculptured principally at the suture with interrupted spiral furrows, shining yellow or reddish-brown, adorned with longitudinal bands, formed by coalescent lines, mostly white and porcellaneous; spire small, convexly-conical, obtuse, suture impressed; whorls 4, moderately convex, the last 4 times exceeding the spire, base rounded; aperture moderately oblique, angularly oval, faintly showing within the external bands; peristome simple, straight, slender, white, columellar margin slightly thickened above.

Length 0·74; *diameter* 0·45 *of an inch.*
Habitat. Port Lincoln, South Australia.—*Masters.*

The coalescent porcellaneous bands, on a darker ground, constitute the most prominent feature of this pretty species, whose nearest ally is *B. trilineatus* of Western Australia.

Genus
ACHATINELLA.—Swainson.

Shell bulimoid, columella generally with a twisted conical or lamelliform tooth.

XXXVI.—SECTION FRICKELLA. *Pfr.* Vers. p. 166.

Sub-perforate, oblong; wall of the aperture furnished with a plate entering spirally inwards; columellar fold compressed, central; peristome simple, straight.

* A. Jacksonensis. * A. Wakefieldiæ.

188. Achatinella Jacksonensis. *Cox.* Plate XII. Fig. 15, *natural size and magnified.* M.C.

Bulimus Jacksonensis. *Cox, Catalogue of Australian Land Shells*, p. 25, 1864.

Shell sub-perforate, oblong turreted, very thin, translucent, rather shining, smooth, under the lens shewing faint longitudinal striæ, yellowish-horny; spire elongated, gradually tapering, rather blunt at the apex; whorls 5 to 6, slightly convex, last equalling ½ of the length; aperture irregularly ovate, with a thin central, vertical, parietal plate; columella twisted, its edge entering spirally inwards, leaving above it a deep entering groove or channel; peristome simple, acute.

Length 0·14; *breadth* 0·06; *aperture* 0·05 *long, of an inch.*

Habitat. Darling Point, and other places about Port Jackson. Wollongong, &c.—*MacGillivray*.

This inconspicuous little horny-brown shell I placed provisionally with *Bulimus*, when describing it three years ago. The curious twisted columella, and the parietal plate, were duly noticed in the original description. They are not compatible with *Bulimus*. On again taking up the subject, I find that the species under consideration comes within the section *Frickella* of the genus *Achatinella*. As all the hitherto recorded species of that genus—210 in 1859, according to Pfeiffer's *Mon. Hel. Viv.*, Vol. IV., p. 570.—are peculiar to the Sandwich Islands, it is a matter of extreme interest to find even an aberrant form, previously known by one species only, represented in Australia.

189. Achatinella Wakefieldiæ. *Cox.* M.C.

Shell imperforate, ovately-conical, very thin, translucent, rather shining, smooth, microscopically striated, yellowish-horny; spire conical, obtuse at the apex; whorls 4, slightly convex, last large, tumid, equalling ½ of the length; aperture irregularly ovate, with a very thin central, vertical, parietal plate; columella thinly expanded and revolute inwards, grooved above; peristome simple, acute.

Length 0·10; *breadth* 0·07; *aperture* 0·05 *long, of an inch.*

Habitat. Grafton, Clarence River, in decaying wood.—*Wakefield*. Ballina, Richmond River, on flowers and leaves of *Hibiscus*.—*Ramsay*.

A very distinct species, differing from the preceding in form, number of whorls, relative length of last whorl, &c.

GENUS
PUPA.—LAMARCK.

Shell rimate or perforate, cylindrical, ovate or bulimiformed; last whorl in proportion small; aperture somewhat irregular, semi-oval or roundish, toothless or dentate; peristome somewhat simple or expanded, margins equal, somewhat parallel, distant, mostly united by a callous lamina.

Animal with a short foot, pointed behind; lower tentacles short. Mandibles finely striated, not rostrate, slightly arcuate; margins concave, entire, in the middle generally slightly prominent. Lingual teeth of the usual form, and moderately numerous.

XXXVII.—SECTION VERTIGO. *Müller*.

Shell minute, sometimes sinistral, ovate, apex acuminate, obtuse; whorls 5 to 6, last rounded; aperture large, semi-oval with 4 to 7 folds; peristome scarcely expanded, white lipped.

Animal with the oral tentacles rudimentary or obsolete.

* P. Australis.   * P. Kingi.   * P. Nelsoni.
* P. Strangei.   * P. Lincolniensis. * P. Margaretæ.
                     * P. Moretonensis.

190. Pupa Australis.

Vertigo Australis. *Adams and Angas, Pro. Zool Soc.*, 1863, p. 522.
Shell sinistral, apex obtuse, umbilicately fissured, pale brown; whorls 7, convex, obliquely strongly striated; aperture semi-ovate, with one parietal and one columellar fold; peristome thickened and widely dilated.
Length 2; breadth ¾ lines.
Habitat. Rapid Bay, S. Australia, in crevices of rocks.—*Angas.*
Copied from the source quoted above. Angas remarks of it—a cylindrical, and, for the genus, a large species, with the aperture furnished with but two plicæ.

191. Pupa Kingi. *Cox.* Plate XIV. Fig. 17, 17 a. M.C.

Cox, Catalogue of Australian Land Shells, p. 28, 1864.
Pupa Mastersi. *Cox, Catalogue of Australian Land Shells*, p. 29, 1864.
Shell sinistral, perforate, shortly cylindrically elliptical, very finely striated, thin, not shining, deep reddish-chestnut horny; spire roundly obtuse; whorls 4, rather convex, last ⅓ of shell; aperture large, somewhat four sided, truncated obliquely, irregularly constricted, furnished with three teeth—one, the largest and most acute on the wall of the aperture; a second, smaller, wider, and obtuse on the columella; and a third, the smallest, and deepest on the outer lip; peristome occasionally slightly thickened and expanded, indented in the centre of outer lip under a sinuation.
Length 0·07; breadth 0·04 of an inch.
Habitat. Parramatta, N. S. W.—*King.* Wollongong.—*Masters.* Globe Point, Sydney.—*Brazier.*
The chestnut-horny colour, indented outer lip, together with the peculiarities of the dentition, render this a well marked species.

192. Pupa Nelsoni. *Cox.* Plate XIV. Fig. 19, 19 a. M.C.

Shell sinistral, perforate, elliptically cylindrical, thin, smooth, microscopically striated, horny reddish-yellow, slightly shining; spire slowly narrowing, obtusely rounded; whorls 5 to 6, slightly convex, last about ½ the length of the shell; aperture, large, rounded, truncated above, with a conspicuous lamelliform tooth on the wall of the aperture, and another, or tubercular callosity, sometimes larger, but obsolete in young specimens at the columellar junction; peristome and teeth white, former expanded, especially at the columella, and not obstructing the minute umbilical opening at the bottom of a deep fissure.
Length 0·15; breadth 0·07; aperture 0·05 long, of an inch.
Habitat. Nelson Bay, near Sydney, N. S. W.—*King.*

193. Pupa Strangei. *Pfr.* Plate XIV. Fig. 15, 15 a. *left variety.* Fig. 18, 18 a. *right variety.* M.C.
Pfr., *Pro. Zool. Soc.*, 1852, p. 69.

Shell dextral or sinistral, fissured, elliptically oblong, thin, not shining, very faintly striated, white, hyaline; spire convexly turreted, apex roundly obtuse; whorls 5, convex, last about ⅔ of the shell, compressed in front; aperture oval, obliquely truncated, with 7 teeth, 2 lamellated close together on the wall of the aperture, 2 on the columella, and 3 more deeply situated within the outer and basal margin; peristome expanded, white, as are the teeth.
Length 0·11; *breadth* 0·05 *of an inch.*
Habitat. Garden Island, Port Jackson.—*Strange.* Clyde River, Parramatta, Port Stephen, and many localities in the vicinity of Sydney, as Darling and Glebe Points, Lyndhurst, Chatsworth, South Creek, N. S. W.—*Masters.*

A dextral variety of this species differs in no essential character, fig. 18, 18 a. Near the sea the specimens seem to be almost universally sinistral, while more inland the reverse is the case, sinistrals being rare.

194. Pupa Lincolniensis. *Cox.* Plate XIV. Fig. 16.
Vertigo Lincolniensis. *Cox*, *Pro. Zool. Soc.*, 1867.

Shell sinistral, rimate, elliptically-oblong, very finely obliquely striated, whitish or rufous horny; spire obtuse; whorls 4 to 6, rather convex, last by no means equalling the rest; aperture almost vertical, lunately-circular; peristome thickened, expanded, white, margins distant, columellar margin straight, sinistral margin above obtusely angled; body whorl centrically armed with a prominent, obtuse, white tooth.
Length 0·13; *diameter* 0·08 *of an inch.*
Habitat. Port Lincoln, South Australia.—*Masters.*

195. Pupa Margaretæ. *Cox.* Plate XIV. Fig. 20, 20 a. *much magnified.* Australian Museum.

Shell dextral, yellowish-brown, minutely perforate, oval, under the lens closely and finely striated, opaque; whorls 5, convex, the last equalling ½ the length of the shell; suture shallow; aperture squarely-oval, having 5 teeth (plicæ), 1 large and unequally divided, situated in the centre of the last whorl, with the points separated, a 2nd sharp and pointed, opposite to the first bifid tooth, and a 3rd and a 4th on the columellar side between the 1st and 2nd—the one nearest the columella being thick and blunt, almost a rounded projection, the other is short and sharp; a 5th, situated between the first two, inserted near the junction of the peristome with the body whorl, is short and thick at the base; peristome thickened, dilated, and reflected, smooth and white, as also are the teeth, margins joined by a broad thick callus, forming with the peristome a continuous circle.
Diameter 0·06; *length* 0·13 *of an inch.*
Habitat. Wallaroo, S. Australia.—*Masters.*

196. Pupa Moretonensis. *Cox.* Plate XIV. Fig. 21, 21 a. *much magnified.* Australian Museum.

Shell small, dextral, sub-perforate, ovate, faintly obliquely striated, yellowish-horny, apex obtuse; whorls 4½, rounded, the last equalling more than half the length of the shell; suture deep and broad; aperture squarely-oval, longer than broad, having four teeth (plicæ) —1 large and bifid, placed closely together, each pointed, the points divergent, situated in the centre of the aperture on the body whorl; a 2nd, longer and thicker, directly opposite to the bifid one; a 3rd near the columella, midway between the other two, short and pointed, thickened at and about its base; a 4th less prominent, and directly opposite to the last, the whole dividing the aperture into 4 equal parts; peristome thickened, broadly and irregularly expanded, smooth and white, as also are the teeth; margins joined by a broad thick callus, continuous with the peristome.

Diameter 0·06; *length* 0·11 *of an inch.*
Habitat. Moreton Bay, Queensland.—*Masters.*

Genus
BALEA.—Prideaux.

Shell turreted, conical, or clavate, slender, usually sinistral, many whorled; aperture semi-oval, or slightly pyriformed; peristome acute, expanded, margins unequal; wall of the aperture with one slight plait; columella simple or transversely plicate; jaw not contracted.

Animal like *Helix*; teeth 20·20; rows 130, *Thomson*; mandibles finely striated, not rostrate.

XXXVIII.—SECTION TEMESA. *Pfr.* Vers. p. 179.

* B. Australis.

197. Balea Australis. *Forbes.* Plate XII. Fig. 16 *natural size,* 16 a. *magnified.* M.C.
Forbes, Voy. of Rattlesnake, Vol. II., p. 380. *Mall.* Pl. II. Fig. 9.

Shell perforated, dextral, cylindrically turreted, decollated, rather thin, with close, prominent, raised riblets along the line of growth, dead white, covered with a yellowish epidermis; whorls 11, rather flattened, last sub-angular beneath the middle; aperture nearly vertical, angularly ovate, and sharply angled above and below, constricted above the middle, within fleshy brown, shining; peristome continuous, thickened, expanded, right margin above slightly impressed, columella nearly straight, with one or two small callosities inside, one like a fold, angular above, then concave, and on centre of the apertural wall a prominent plate projects and extends spirally out of sight.

Length 0·70; width 0·16; aperture 0·17 long; broad 0·11 of an inch.

Habitat. Port Molle, Queensland.—*MacGillivray.* Miriam Vale, Port Curtis, Queensland.—*Blackman.*

The description applies to specimens from the latter locality, with fully formed mouths; I cannot find that the "three folded columella" of Forbes' original description agrees with mine, unless he has intended the plait on the body whorl to be the *superior* on the columella, and by misprint *inferior* has been given.

GENUS

VITRINA.—DRAPARNAUD.

Shell imperforate, very thin, pellucid, hyaline, depressed; spire short; whorls 2 to 3, rapidly enlarging; aperture large, lunate or rounded, columellar margin slightly inflected; peristome thin, often membranous.

Animal elongated, too large for complete retraction into the shell; mantle produced, transversely rugose, covering the front edge of the last whorl and part of the spire of the shell, and furnished with a posterior lobe on the right side. Mandibles arcuate, rostrate; lingual teeth (of type, *Vitrina Draparnaudi*), 100 rows of 75 each; marginal teeth with a single, long, recurved apex.—*Thomson.*

I may here remark that the animals of all the Australian *Vitrinæ* have more the characters of *Arion*, the tail being longer, more abruptly truncated, the mantle more developed and possessing a *caudal gland.*

* V. Milligani.	* V. Freycineti.	* V. leucospira.
* V. Verreauxi.	* V. castanea.	* V. robusta.
* V. nigra.	* V. Strangei.	* V. hyalina.
* V. virens.	* V. inflata.	* V. Mastersi.
* V. MacGillivrayi.	* V. megastoma.	* V. Australis.

198. Vitrina Milligani. *Pfr.* Plate XIV. Fig. 2, 2 a. M.C. *Pfr., Pro. Zool. Soc.*, 1852, p. 56.

Shell depressly-ovate, rather solid, polished, very glossy, translucent, olive black; spire convex; whorls 3, 2nd convex, last depressly rounded; aperture more oblique than diagonal, lunately rounded-

oval, within coloured as without; peristome simple, right margin dilated forwards, anterior regularly, and columella slightly arched.
Diameter, greatest 0·83; *least* 0·60; *height* 0·35; *aperture* 0·45 *long*; 0·45 *broad, of an inch.*
Habitat. Island in Macquarie Harbour, Tasmania.—*Milligan.*
This remarkable, shining, and nearly black *Vitrina* resembles in a most striking manner very young specimens of *Helix Busbyi*, of New Zealand, but, like all others of the genus, is imperforate.

199. Vitrina Freycineti. *Fer.* Plate XIV. Fig. 4, 4 a. M.C.
Pfr., Pro. Zool. Soc., 1849, p. 132.
Reeve, Conc. Icon. sp. 21.

Shell depressed, very thin, diaphanous, smooth, shining, very faintly plicately striated; spire minute, not projecting, suture impressed, faintly margined; whorls 3½, enlarging rapidly, last rather narrow at the base, rather depressed above, less so below; aperture large, elliptically lunate; peristome simple.
Diameter, greatest 0·65; *least* 0·40; *height* 0·25; *aperture* 0·40 *long*; 0·32 *broad, of an inch.*
Habitat. Lane Cove, N. S. W.
Reeve remarks of this, that it is distinguished chiefly by its narrowly produced transverse form.

200. Vitrina leucospira. *Pfr.* Plate XIV. Fig. 6, *copied from Reeve.*
Pfr., Pro. Zool. Soc., 1856, p. 326.
Reeve, Conc. Icon. sp. 42.

Shell depressly sub-globular, outline oval, very thin, slightly striated, pellucid, shining, yellowish hyaline; spire scarcely convex, white; suture hardly margined; whorls 4, slightly convex, third perceptibly pellucidly radiate, last rounded; aperture oblique, lunately sub-circular; peristome thin, margins converging, somewhat inflected, right strongly arched in front, columella nearly straight, short, thread-like.
Diameter, greatest 0·53; *least* 0·45; *height* 0·33 *of an inch.*
Habitat. Australia.
Not having seen a specimen of this most globular of Australian *Vitrinæ*, I have drawn upon Pfeiffer—*Mon. Hel. Viv.*, Vol. IV., p. 796. Reeve says it is globose, and but little depressed, thin, sub-membranous, with the apex opaque, milky white. I may observe that this kind of white apex is occasionally met with in other species, and frequently in *V. Strangei*.

201. Vitrina Verreauxi. *Pfr.* Plate XIV. Fig. 14, 14 a. M.C.
Pfr., Pro. Zool. Soc., 1849, p. 132.
Reeve, Conc. Icon. sp. 21.

Shell depressly auriform, thin, diaphanous, slightly shining, smooth, frequently rugosely striated at the suture, faintly elsewhere; spire nearly flat, suture impressed, narrowly margined; whorls 3, the last depressed above, produced, rounded at the periphery and below;

aperture diagonal, lunately ovate; peristome simple, sharp, right margin curved forwards, then gradually rounding to the columellar margin, which is membranous.

Diameter, greatest 0·55; *least* 0·45; *height* 0·17; *aperture, length* 0·40; *breadth* 0·35 *of an inch*.

Habitat. Australia.—*Verreaux*. Mount Wellington. North West Coast, and elsewhere in Tasmania.

Reeve says this is chiefly distinguished by its narrowly produced transverse form; but this, it must be recollected, is to a much less degree than the words would imply. My Tasmanian specimens, including 3 from Cuming, marked *V. Verreauxi, B. Tasmania*, agree with Pfeiffer's description; but in it there is no mention made of the membranous columellar margin.

202. Vitrina castanea. *Pfr.* Plate XIV. Fig. 11, *copied from Reeve.*

Pfr., Pro. Zool. Soc., 1851, p. 56.
Reeve, Conc. Icon. sp. 37.

Shell depressed, with the periphery ovate, slightly striated, very polished, chestnut coloured; spire flat; whorls 3, scarcely convex, the last large, with a broad membranous edge beneath; aperture a little oblique, lunate oval; peristome with a yellow stripe behind its membranous margin.

Diameter, greatest 0·35; *least* 0·27; *height* 0·20 *of an inch.*
Habitat. Australia.—*Verreaux.*

To the preceding description taken from Pfeiffer may be added, that Reeve alludes to it as a bright transparent shell, of a rich chestnut olive hue.

203. Vitrina robusta. *Gould.*

Gould, Pro. Boston Soc., 1846.
Expedition Shells. Pl. I. Fig. 11.

Shell helicoid, transverse, depressed and globose, rather strong, polished, very bright, pale yellowish-green, striated with regular, obtuse, lines of growth; spire obtuse; whorls 3, the last large; apex sub-central, rounded beneath; aperture rounded, left margin reflected above, forming a small umbilical fissure.

Breadth ½, *axis* ¼ *of an inch. From the figure—greater diameter* 0·60; *lesser diameter* 0·40; *alt.* 0·31 *of an inch.*
Habitat. East Coast of Australia.—*Gould.*

The preceding is Gould's description from Pfeiffer, in *Brit. Mus. Cat. of Pulm.*, p. 69. It seems to me that this is in no respect different from that named *V. Strangei* three years afterwards.

204. Vitrina nigra. *Quoy et Gaimard.*

Quoy et Gaimard, Voy. d'Astrol., Zool., Vol. II., p. 135. Pl. XI. Fig. 8—9.

Shell oval, rather flattened, reddish; aperture elliptical, ample, left margin slightly inflected; whorls 4, the last very large.

Diameter 6; *height* 2½ *lines (French).*

Habitat. Port Western, Victoria.—*Quoy et Gaimard.*
The preceding is taken from Quoy, who remarks that the animal is black, large, with an elongate neck, and contractile into the shell.

205. Vitrina Strangei. *Pfr.* Plate XIV. Fig. 9, 9 a. *large variety.* Plate XIV. Fig. 3, 3 a. *small variety.*
Pfr., Pro. Zool. Soc., 1849, p. 132.
Reeve, Conc. Icon. sp. 48.

Shell depressly semi-globose, thin, smooth, transparent, very faintly arcuately striated, more conspicuously at the suture, and sometimes, under the lens, shewing indications of spiral impressed lines, golden, yellowish, greenish, or pale hyaline; spire small, slightly prominent, suture impressed, slightly bordered; whorls 3, slightly convex, rapidly increasing, last depressed above, rounded outwardly, and more convex below; aperture oblique, large, lunate, rounded; peristome simple, rather blunt, margins approximating, right dilated forwards, columella receding, much curved, with a narrow membranacious margin.
Diameter, greatest 0.65; *least* 0.45; *height* 0.25; *aperture* 0.40 *long*; 0.37 *wide, of an inch.*
Habitat. Cook's River. Lane Cove. Mulgoa. Dural. Clarence and Richmond Rivers, N. S. W. Brisbane. Fitzroy River, Queensland.—*Cox.*

A shell so widely distributed might be expected to present many variations, yet it does not, excepting those of mere size, colour, and degree of transparency; almost universally, however, it is a beautifully bright, clear, transparent shell.

206. Vitrina hyalina. *Pfr.* Plate XIV. Fig. 7, 7 a. M.C.
Pfr., Pro. Zool. Soc., 1854, p. 296.

Shell depressly-globose, very thin, smooth, pellucid, greenish hyaline; spire slightly elevated, slightly obtuse; whorls, nearly 4, slightly convex, last smooth towards the suture, which is margined, distantly radiately striated, rounded at the base, rather wide; aperture diagonal, lunately rounded; peristome simple, right margin rather dilated in front, columella very much arched.
Diameter, greatest 0.27; *least* 0.21; *height* 0.14 *of an inch.*
Habitat. Moreton Bay.—*Strange.*

The smallest recorded Australian species, found, I believe, on trees. Specimens of a small leaf-inhabiting *Vitrina* from Queensland and the Richmond River, and also Elizabeth Bay in the vicinity of Sydney, in my collection, I refer, but not with certainty, to this species. The whorls in the largest are not more than 3; the spire is not elevated, and the columellar margin is membranous. I may add that they are not the young of other species.

207. Vitrina virens. *Pfr.* Plate XIV. Fig. 5, 5 a. M.C.
Pfr., Pro. Zool. Soc., 1848, p. 108.
Reeve, Conc. Icon. sp. 14.

Shell depressed, somewhat broadly ear-shaped, or roundly elliptical, very faintly striated, rather solid for the genus, dull greenish-olive; spire rather flattened; whorls 3, very slightly convex, rapidly increasing, last depressly rounded; aperture lunately-roundish; peristome thin, decliningly curved above, regularly arcuate in front, columella curved below, and nearly straight above, minutely reflexed to form an umbilical fissure.

Diameter, greatest 0·70; least 0·50; height 0·20; aperture 0·40 long; 0·37 broad of an inch.

Habitat. Moreton Bay, Queensland. Clarence River, N. S. W.—*MacGillivray.*

208. Vitrina inflata. *Reeve.* Plate XIV. Fig. 1, *copied from Reeve.*

Reeve, Conc. Icon. sp. 64.

Shell ovately ear-shaped, yellowish-horny, but little shining; spire small, scarcely emerged; whorls convex, inflated, thinly arcuately striated; aperture rather largely openly ovate.

Habitat. Sydney.—*Mrs. Cuming.*

Reeve, whose description has been copied, further states, that notwithstanding the close affinity of many species of this form of *Vitrina*, he is unable to refer the present to any previously described. It has a peculiarly inflated open-mouthed character. Measurements are not given, and the figure is an enlarged one.

209. Vitrina Mastersi. *Cox.* Plate XIV. Fig. 12, 12 a. M.C.

Shell depressed, very thin, smooth, transparent, extremely shining, very finely curvately striated, with a few faint spiral lines, bright golden yellow with occasionally a greenish tinge; spire very slightly prominent, apex central, suture impressed, narrowly margined; whorls 3, slightly convex, last rather depressed, rounded at the periphery, and rather convex beneath on outer half; aperture diagonal, lunately ovate; peristome simple, right margin slightly dilated above and in front, left rather straightly continuous with the columella, which is strongly arcuate above, the left margin and base membranous and flattened.

Diameter, greatest 0·55; least 0·38; height 0·17; aperture 0·35 long; 0·27 broad, of an inch.

Habitat. Kiama, N. S. W.—*Masters.*

A delicate bright golden-yellow hyaline shell, allied to *V. Strangei*, but easily distinguished by being much more depressed, and having half of the base membranous. The animal of this shell is whitish, and not grey as in *V. Strangei.*

210. Vitrina MacGillivrayi. *Cox.* Plate XIV. Fig. 8, 8 a. M.C.

Vitrina planilabris. *Cox, Pro. Zool. Soc.*, 1865, p. 697.

Shell ear-shaped, very much depressed, thin, translucent, polished, clothed with an olive-green epidermis, shortly striated, and under the lens are seen a few spiral depressed lines; spire very small, scarcely prominent, nucleus whitish; whorls 3, the last very large,

flatly convex exteriorly; aperture lunately-ovate, pearly within; peristome thin, columellar margin very thin, flat, keeled without.
Diameter, greatest 0·80; *least* 0·50; *height* 0·26; *aperture* 0·55 *long*; 0·42 *wide, of an inch.*
Habitat. Mitchell River.—*Porter.* Urara River, New South Wales.—*MacGillivray.*
This species is large and very much depressed. It is easily distinguished by the flatness of the base of the shell along the inner lip. The animal when disturbed exudes a secretion of a purple colour. Young shells show great tumidity of the body whorl.

211. Vitrina megastoma. *Cox.* Plate XIV. Fig. 13, 13 a.

Shell depressed, of a longish auriform, smooth, very thin, transparent, greenish, shining, very faintly striated; spire not prominent; whorls 3, slightly convex, last, depressed above, rounded at the periphery and below; aperture very large, oblique, lunately-ovate; peristome regular, right margin rather straight, then arched in front, and after this less curved to the middle of the columella where it becomes arched; left margin and base of the shell membranous, flattened.
Diameter, greatest 0·45; *least* 0·30; *height* 0·10; *aperture* 0·35 *long*; 0·26 *broad, of an inch.*
Habitat. Clarence River.—*MacGillivray.*
An elongated bright greenish-yellow hyaline shell, remarkable for the narrowness of the last whorl below, and the large size of the aperture. To a certain extent it exhibits a transition to the *Section Peltella*, represented by the next species, *V. Australis*.

212. Vitrina Australis. *Pfr. M.* Plate XIV. Fig. 10, copied from Reeve.

Reeve, Conc. Icon. sp. 70.
Shell very depressly ear-shaped, open at the base, yellowish-horny; spire small, rather immersed; whorls impressed at the sutures, faintly arcuately plicately striated, membranous at the edge.
Habitat. Eastern Australia.—*Reeve.*
The above has been taken from Reeve.
This species is an example of a *Section Peltella*, which differs from others of the genus in having only a portion of the whorls formed; the base of the shell next the animal is open or too membranous to be preserved.

Genus
SUCCINEA.—Draparnaud.

Shell imperforate, thin, ovate or oblong; spire very small; aperture large, obliquely oval; columella simple, acute, straight; peristome simple, acute, straight.

Animal amphibious, large, heliciform; tentacles short

and thick, upper ones of even thickness towards the apex, thence attenuated; foot broad; lingual teeth like *Helix*; *Succinea putris* has 50 rows of 65 teeth each.—*Thomson*.

* S. Australis.   * S. strigata.   * S. scalarina.
* S. strigillata. * S. arborea.   * S. Eucalypti.
* S. Nortoni.   * S. MacGillivrayi. * S. aperta.
                * S. Menkeana.

213. Succinea Australis. *Fer.* Plate XV. Fig. 7, 7 a. M.C.
Ferussac, Hist. Moll. Pl. XII. Fig. 11.

Shell ovately-conical, thin, rugosely striated, pellucid, pale horny, sometimes marked with darker streaks; spire conical, acute; whorls 3½, convex, last forming 2-3rd of the length, columella sub-callous, somewhat slightly receding; aperture acuminately oval, incumbent; peristome simple, straight.

Length 0·47; *breadth* 0·32; *aperture* 0·32 *long*; 0·20 *broad, of an inch.*
Habitat. Tasmania.—*Cuna.*

For the purpose of serving as a starting point, and to determine the identity of this the first mentioned of Australian *Succineæ*, I have copied Pfeiffer's description, taking the measurements from my own specimens. Perhaps "acutely" had better be substituted for "acuminately;" I cannot count more than 3 whorls, the number represented in Ferussac's figure.

When Ferussac named and described this species, he gave as its habitat "Australian Isles." Quoy and Gaimard afterwards found in Tasmania a *Succinea*, which they also referred to *S. Australis*, and figured and described it. Of course, neither their descriptions nor figures agree perfectly. Pfeiffer, many years afterwards, having previously in 1848 pointed out the discrepancy between the figures, in 1859—*Mon. Hel. Viv.*, Vol. IV., p. 812—gives an original description of *S. Australis* from Tasmanian specimens, with which certain of those in my collection agree. It may be mentioned here, in case it should be supposed that New Caledonia is included in the range of this species, that in the "*Faun. Conch, &c., de la Nouvelle Caledonia,*" by M. Ganies, the figure given from a New Caledonian specimen is that of another species, as one glance at the left lip will show, while the description is Pfeiffer's, verbatim, from Tasmanian specimens.

In Menke's specimen, "*Molluscorum Novæ Hollandiæ,*" he records, p. 6, the existence of *Succinea amphibia*, of Drap., as occurring under the bark of Eucalypti, in the district of Hay, W. Australia, and *S oblonga*, Drap., in the fissures of calcareous rocks, not far from the sea, near Perth, Western Australia. The first of these is by Pfeiffer looked on as a synonym of *S. putris*, Lin., and like the latter is believed to be confined to Europe.

214. Succinea strigata. *Pfr.* Plate XV. Fig. 1, 1 a. *dark variety*, 2 *light variety, enlarged.* M.C.
Pfr., Pro. Zool. Soc., 1854, p. 297.
Succinea rhodostoma. *Cox, Catalogue of Australian Land Shells*, 1864.

Shell ovately acuminate, thin, opaque, slightly shining, longitudinally and irregularly striated, whitish, yellowish, or reddish-horny, with occasional pale streaks; spire conical, acute, papillary; whorls 3, convex, last inflated; the aperture slightly exceeding the spire, scarcely oblique, irregularly and narrowly ovate, enamelled within of general colour of shell; peristome simple, thin, columella very narrow, whitely callous.
Length 0·45; *breadth* 0·23; *aperture* 0·25 *long*; 0·20 *broad, of an inch.*
Habitat. Port Lincoln, Point Lowly, Wallaroo, Flinder's Range, Penola, S. Australia.—*Angas, Masters, Woods, &c.*

The above description exhibits the ordinary and average appearance of this shell, which, however, attains to greater dimensions. A large white variety from Wallaroo is remarkable. Mr. Masters informed me that this species, which he found in every place he visited in South Australia, does not confine itself to the ground, but is equally found on trees.

215. Succinea scalarina. *Pfr.*
Pfr., Pro. Zool. Soc., 1861, p. 28.

Shell ovately-conical, "scalarina," rather solid, irregularly rugosely plicated, slightly shining, reddish; spire elongated, rather acute; whorls 3½, convex, last slightly exceeding the spire, somewhat attenuated at the base; columella receding, nearly straight, forming with the peristome an indistinct angle; aperture oblique, oval, scarcely angular above; peristome simple, columellar margin slightly reflected above.
Diameter, greatest 0·51; *least* 0·30; *height* 0·21 *of an inch.*
Habitat. King George's Sound, W. Australia.—*Angas.*

The preceding description has been entirely taken from Pfeiffer. It will be seen by the measurements to be one of the largest Australian species. *Scalarina* may be translated as resembling a staircase—but conchological latin is not always to be found in a dictionary.

216. Succinea strigillata. *Adams and Angas.* Plate XV.
Fig 5, 5 a. *enlarged.* M.C.
Adams and Angas, Pro. Zool. Soc., 1864, p. 38.

Shell ovately conical, thin, semi-pellucid, pale horny yellow; spire scarcely equalling the aperture, apex papillary; whorls 3½, strongly convex, longitudinally, finely and minutely striated; aperture oblong ovate, left margin with a long thin callous deposit, right simple.
Length 5 lines; breadth 2½ *lines.*
Habitat. Shark's Bay, N. W. Australia.—*Angas.*

The authors from whom the description has been taken remark that it is somewhat allied to *S. strigata*, having the same papillary apex, but differing in being smaller, thinner, of a lighter colour, and in the whorls being less strongly rugose.

217. Succinea arborea. *Adams and Angas.*
Adams and Angas, Pro. Zool. Soc., 1863, p. 523.

Shell oblong ovate; spire shorter than the aperture, apex papillary, white, golden horny, pellucid; whorls 3, strongly convex, longi-

tudinally "strigosis" (qu. strigatis-furrowed?); aperture oblong ovate, left lip furnished with a thin callus, right lip simple, arched.
Length 4 *lines; breadth* 2 *lines.*
Habitat. Burnside, and hills near Adelaide, S. Australia, beneath bark of gum trees.—*Angas.*

Not having seen specimens of this small species, I have been obliged to copy the original description. It is stated to be as strictly arboreal, as *S. strigata* is terrestrial.

218. Succinea Eucalypti. *Cox.* Plate XV. Fig. 3, 3 a. *enlarged*, 3 b. *on bark.* M.C.
Cox, *Pro. Zool. Soc.*, 1864, p.

Shell ovate, thin, shining, translucent, smooth, very faintly and irregularly striated, pale reddish-horny; spire very short, obtuse and papillary at the apex; whorls 3, convex, last ovate; aperture about twice the length of the spire, of a nearly regular oval, very slightly oblique, within thinly enamelled and glossy; peristome simple, straight, margins connected by thin callus, columella nearly straight, receding towards the axis.
Length 0·28; *breadth* 0·17; *aperture* 0·20 *long*; 0·10 *broad, of an inch.*
Habitat. Throughout N. S. W., from the Clyde River on the South, to the Clarence River on the north, New South Wales. Facing Island, Port Curtis, Queensland.—*Cox.*

Although this small species is chiefly found under the bark of gum trees, *Eucalypti*, it is not confined to such situations, but goes out on the branches and leaves of other trees and bushes.

219. Succinea Nortoni. *Cox.* Plate XV. Fig. 4, 4 a. *enlarged.* M.C.
Cox, *Catalogue of Australian Land Shells*, 1864, p. 27.

Shell ovate, thin, extremely ventricose, pellucid, horny, apex reddish; whorls 4, roughly and irregularly longitudinally ribbed, last very largely inflated; aperture ovate; peristome simple, acute; columella simple, straight, acute.
Length 0·47; *breadth* 0·36 *of an inch.*
Habitat. Norton's Basin, Nepean River, N. S. W.—*Cox.*

220. Succinea MacGillivrayi. *Cox.* Plate XV. Fig. 6, 6 a. *enlarged.* M.C.
Cox, *Catalogue of Australian Land Shells*, 1864, p. 27.

Shell ovate, extremely ventricose, dirty brown, apex rose-coloured; whorls 3, under the lens minutely striated; aperture very large, ovate; peristome simple, acute; columella simple, acute, straight.
Length 0·30; *breadth* 0·20 *of an inch.*
Habitat. Mount Henry, Mulgoa, N. S. W., under stones in moist places.—*Cox.*

221. Succinea aperta. *Cox.* Plate XVII. Fig. 6, 6 a., 6 b. *much magnified.* Australian Museum.

Shell oval, very thin, yellowish-horny, pellucid, polished, lightly striated; spire very small, equalling only ⅛ the length of the aperture, conical dull, rose-coloured; whorls 4, convex, the last very largely and openly dilated, suture deep; aperture very large, wide, openly and flatly expanded, giving the shell the appearance of a scoop; peristome simple, columella arched and not thickened by a callus.

Diameter, greatest 0·46; *least* 0·28; *aperture* 0·36 *long*; 0·25 *broad of an inch.*

Habitat. King George's Sound, W. Australia.—*Masters.*

This species may at once be identified by the broad, shallow, flattened out appearance of the last whorl.

222. Succinea Menkeana. *Pfr.*
Pfr., Mon. Hel. Viv., Vol. III., p. 14.
Succinea amphibia. *Menke, Moll. Nov. Holl.*, p. 6.

Shell ovately-elliptical, thin, distinctly striated, pellucid, shining, horny; spire short, papilla-formed, suture deep; whorls $2\frac{1}{2}$, the last but one very convex, the last attenuated at the base; columella somewhat callous, regularly curved; aperture slightly oblique, regularly oval; peristome simple, thin, margins approaching.

Length 0·27; *breadth* 0·14; *height* 0·15; *aperture* 0·19 *long*; 0·11 *broad, of an inch.*

Habitat. New Holland.—*Priess.*

This description is taken from the author above quoted.

Section B.—OPERCULATA.

PNEUMONOPOMA.—Pfeiffer.

Mon. Pneum. Viv., 1852, *Introd.*, p. 1. *Suppl. prim.*, 1858, p. 1. *Suppl. Sec.*, 1865, p. 1.

Terrestrial Mollusca breathing air by lungs, and furnished with an operculum attached to the foot of the animal, by which it closes the aperture of its spiral shell.

All the animals of this order strongly resemble each other in structure, by which, besides the operculum, they are easily distinguished from the other terrestrial Mollusca (*Limacidæ, Helicidæ, Oncidiadæ, Lymnœidæ, Auriculidæ*). The sexes are strictly distinct, never hermaphrodites, as in *Helicea*, and the animals bear 2 contractile, not retractile, tentacles, at whose posterior or exterior bases the eyes are placed. In some the mantle margin is free, by which character Ferussac distinguished the *Helicinæ* from the *Turbines*; in others, the mantle is entirely hidden within the shell.

SUB-ORDER I.—OPISOPHTHALMA. *Pfeiffer*.

Mon. Pneum. Viv., 1852, p. 3. *Suppl. prim.*, 1858, p. 2. *Suppl. Sec*, 1865, p. 1.

Eyes placed on the upper part of the head behind the base of the subulate tentacles; foot rather short.

FAM. I.—ACICULACEA. *Pfeiffer*.

Mon. Pneum. Viv., 1852, p. 3. *Suppl. prim.*, 1858, p. 3. *Suppl Sec*, 1865, p. 1.

Operculum thin, spiral, few whorled.

GENUS
TRUNCATELLA.—Risso.

Shell minute, imperforate, turreted, adult always truncated, sub-cylindrical, smooth or ribbed; aperture oval or elliptical, entire; peristome continuous, straight or slightly expanded, simple or duplicate. Operculum thin, horny, hardly sub-spiral, nucleus basal.

Animal, tentacles two, short, triangularly diverging, cylindrical, obtuse; eyes centrally behind; foot short, rounded at each end; head proboscidiformed, bi-lobed, by which and the short foot the animal is enabled to creep.

* * T. teres.
* * T. Yorkensis.
* * T. marginata.
* * T. Brazieri.
* * T. ferruginea.
* * T. scalarina.
* * T. Pfeifferi.

223. Truncatella teres. *Pfr.* Plate XV. Fig 9 *natural size*, 9 a., 9 b. *much enlarged*. M.C.
Pfr., Proc. Zool. Soc., 1856.

Shell hardly subrimate, cylindrical, rather thin, more or less distinctly longitudinally ribbed, pellucid, shining, reddish-horny; suture margined, strongly plicately-crenated; whorls in the adult state 4, somewhat equal, rather convex, last shortly crested at the base, callous, whitish; aperture vertical, broadly oval, above angulated, towards the right dilated; peristome simple, continuous, right margin rather expanded, attached to the columellar margin.

Length 0·23; breadth 0·07; *aperture obliquely* 0·07 *long, of an inch*.
Habitat. Trinity Bay, N. E. Australia.—*MacGillivray*.
The above is the original description given by Pfeiffer.

224. Truncatella marginata. *Kuster.* Plate XV. Fig. 8 *natural size*, 8 a., 8 b. *much enlarged*. M.C.
Kuster, Mon., p. 12. Sp. 8, p. 2. Fig. 24—26.

Shell subrimate, cylindrical, gradually attenuating upwards, rather thin, shining, amber-colour or pale yellow; suture margined, furnished with papilliformed folds; whorls in the adult state 4 to 4½, rather convex, last with folds at the base, very shortly or obsoletely crested; aperture vertical, angularly oval. somewhat broad at the base; peristome continuous, thin, rather expanded.

Obs. Young shell turreted, apex acute; whorls 8, swollen, ribbed above, last obtusely angled.

Length 0·25; breadth 0·09; aperture about 0·07 long, of an inch.

Habitat. Port Lincoln, S. Australia, very plentiful.—*Masters.*

225. Truncatella scalarina. Cox. Plate XV. Fig. 10 *natural size*, 10 a., 10 b. *much enlarged.* M.C.

Cox, Pro. Zool. Soc., 1867, p. 40.

Shell imperforate, fusiformly turreted, smooth, shining, white; spire decollated, suture constricted; whorls 4 at the least, convex, strongly longitudinally and regularly ribbed, last equalling in length the three preceding ones; aperture oblique, oblongly-ovate; peristome continuous, free, callous, expanded, especially above, exhibiting underneath a bilabiated form, right margin curved, rounded below, superior margin nearly straight; operculum?

Length 0·23; breadth 0·11 of an inch.

Habitat. Port Lincoln, in great abundance.—*Masters.*

This remarkable shell, reminding one somewhat of a *scalaria*, occurs in a semi-fossil state in the same district where the recent smaller and smoother *T. marginata*, Küster, appears to be plentiful.

226. Truncatella Yorkensis. Cox. Plate XV. Fig. 11 *natural size*, 11 a., 11 b. *much enlarged.* M.C.

Shell scarcely rimate, cylindrical, attenuated, rather thin, ribs dull pale-yellow, scarcely waving, very slightly elevated, smooth, with the interstices diaphanous, chalky white and equi-distant, suture indented; whorls in the adult state 4, slightly convex, last elongated: aperture vertical, large and broadly oval, angled above; peristome white, continuous, slightly thickened, straight, columellar margin expanded and moderately reflected; operculum?

Length 0·34; breadth 0·13; aperture 0·08 long, of an inch.

Habitat. Cape York, N. E. Australia.—*Damel.*

This species may be distinguished by its fine straight shining ribs with chalky interstices, and its pure white mouth.

227. Truncatella Brazieri. Cox. Plate XV. Fig. 12 *natural size*, 12 a., 12 b. *much enlarged.* M.C

Shell rimate, cylindrical, sub-attenuated, solid, ribs elevated, rather straight, large, and widely separated, the interstices longitudinally striated, reddish-yellow; whorls in the adult state 4, rather convex, gradually increasing in size, suture margined; aperture oval; peristome continuous, thickened; columellar margin straight, thickened, and reflected; operculum?

Length 0·27; breadth 0·10; aperture 0·09 long, of an inch.

Habitat. Miller's Point, Sydney, N. S. W., one foot above high water mark, living under wood.—*Brazier.*

This species is easily recognised by the broad sculptured interstices between the well defined ribs, and by its margined suture. I have named it after my friend, Mr. John Brazier, to whose care and perseverance in collecting, this and many other rare species of land and marine Mollusca have been added to our Australian fauna.

228. Truncatella Pfeifferi. *Martens.* Museum, Mr. Brazier.
Martens, in Malac. Bl., Vol. VIII., p. 43, 1860.

Shell rimate, shortly sub-cylindrical, slightly attenuated upwards, rather solid, ribs somewhat straight, interstices equi-distant, in the last whorl the sculpture disappears, yellow; suture indented; whorls in the adult state 4½, rather convex, last rounded at the base, shortly descending; aperture vertical, oval, not widened at the base; peristome continuous, straight, obtuse.

Length 0·23; *breadth* 0·11; *aperture* 0·07 *long, of an inch.*
Habitat. Shark Island, Port Jackson, Sydney, New South Wales.—*Brazier.*

The above is Martens description, as given by Pfeiffer, of this species, the original specimens of which were found in Japan.

229. Truncatella ferruginea. *Cox.* M.C.

Shell sub-rimate, rather solid, cylindrical, tapering, truncate, dull reddish, costulate, ribs numerous, much raised, regular, scarcely waving, interstices smooth; whorls 4, gradually increasing, suture deep, not puckered; aperture vertical, oval, pointed above; peristome much thickened, continuous, pale and glossy, columella callous, thickened, continuous with the peristome; operculum?

Length 0·28; *breadth* 0·12; *aperture* 0·08 *of an inch.*
Habitat. Cape York, N. E. Australia.—*Damel.*

FAM. II.—DIPLOMMATINACEA *Pfeiffer.*

Mon. Pneum. Viv., 1858. *Suppl. prim.,* p. 9. *Suppl. Sec.* 1865, p. 8.

Eyes placed on the outer basis of the long filiform tentacles, sessile upon two lobes. Operculum subtestaceous, few whorled.

GENUS

BLANFORDIA.—MENKE?

Operculum horny, paucispiral, with a sub-central nucleus; aperture oval, continuous; shell spiral, umbilicated, decollated.

* B. striatula. * B. pyrrhostoma.

230. Blanfordia striatula. *Menke.* Plate XV. Fig. 13 *natural size*, 13 a., 13 b. *much enlarged*, 13 c. *operculum of same.* M.C. *Menke, Moll. Nov. Holland,* p. 9.

Shell rimate, truncately fusiform, rather smooth, not shining, covered with dull olivaceous epidermis; spire tapering, decollated, suture distinct; whorls in adult state 4, gradually increasing; aperture almost vertical, its axis slightly oblique, elliptical; peristome reddish-brown within, moderately thickened, and on columellar margin expanded, leaving uncovered a small umbilical fissure; operculum black, horny, 3—4 spiral.

Length 0·33; *breadth* 0·17; *aperture* 0·07 *long, of an inch.*

Habitat. Adelaide, South Australia. Tasmania.—*Angas.* Botanic Gardens, Melbourne, Victoria.—*Brazier.*

I cannot find any clue whatever to the work in which this genus was first published by Menke; in fact my only record of it is a remark by Angas, in *Pro. Zool. Soc.*, 1863, p. 523; and the characters above are taken from specimens in my collection. Pfeiffer, in his Supplement II., 1865, p. 8, of *Pneumonopomorum Viventium,* in alluding to this species, doubts to which genus it belongs.

231. Blanfordia pyrrhostoma. *Cox.* Plate XV. Fig. 14, 14 a. Australian Museum.

Shell rimate, cylindrically tapering, decollated, obsoletely rib-striated, especially on the first whorl, and there decussated with fine spiral lines, dull white without lustre; spire very regularly tapering; whorls, at least, six, uniformly slightly convex, last convex; aperture slightly oblique, its axis divergent from that of the shell, nearly elliptical; peristome white, inside of mouth bright red, enamelled, margins slightly joined by a callus, expanded, especially below and on columellar margin, leaving uncovered a minute umbilical fissure and aperture.

Length 0·70; *breadth* 0·30; *aperture* 0·20 *long, of an inch.*

Habitat. Sharks Bay, Western Australia.—*Masters.*

The only specimens of this shell (4) which I have seen are in the Australian Museum. All have a dull, dead, semi-fossil chalky look, yet the brightness of the enamelled mouth shews that they are not "dead shells." Probably the number of whorls will be found to be about 9.

Genus

DIPLOMMATINA.—Benson.

Shell minute, dextral or sinistral, thin, conical, whorls costulated, convex, last sub-ascendant; aperture nearly circular; peristome double, outer expanded; operculum thin, horny, round, pauci-spiral with thin prominent laminæ on their external edges.

Animal like *Cyclophorus*.

* D. Bensoni.   ⁵ D. Australiæ.

232. Diplommatina Bensoni. *A. Adams.* Plate XVI. Fig. 1 *natural size*, 1 a., 1 b. *magnified*.   M.C.
A. Adams, Pro. Zool. Soc., 1852, p. 91.

Shell sinistral, imperfectly rimate, cylindrically ovate, pupiform, with regular, distant, oblique, prominent, continuous, or nearly so, ribs crossing the whorls, the interstices under the lens finely transversely striated, white, not shining; whorls convex, 1st papillose, 2nd very much broader, 3rd, 4th, and 5th suddenly enlarging and tumidly convex, 4 and 5 widest and equal, but last projecting more behind, last whorl contracted; aperture vertical, circular; peristome porcellaneously white, outer portion slightly expanded, inner separated by a groove straight, slightly expanded on the right lip.

Length 0·12; *breadth* 0·07 *of an inch.*

Habitat. Moreton Bay, Queensland.—*Strange.*

Two specimens which the Rev. R. L. King has obligingly lent me are marked as from the Clarence River, N. S. W. The rimation or substitute for an umbilical opening is, in this species, confined to a slight shallow hollow. A Norfolk Island species, not yet named, approaches more closely to the present than any of the four Lord Howe Island *Diplommatinæ* described by Pfeiffer, although the latter locality is within a day's steaming of New South Wales, and the former five times as far distant.

233. Diplommatina Australiæ. *Benson.* Plate XVII. Fig. 7, 7 a., 7 b. *much magnified.*   Australian Museum.
Benson, in Ann. and Mag., Nat. His., 2nd Ser., XV., p. 331, 1855.

Shell sinistral, rimate, sub-ovately-conical, glabrous, faintly ribbed, pale horny; spire ovately-conical, apex rather acute; whorls 6, convex, last narrowed, ascending in front; aperture vertical, subcircular; peristome double, posteriorly expanded, anteriorly rather expanded, margins shining, diaphanous, joined by a callus, exterior margin shortly produced above, columellar margin dilated with a tubercle inconspicuous or obsolete. Operculum remote, squarish, plate scarcely raised.

Length 0·13; *breadth scarcely* 0·07 *of an inch.*

Habitat. Mount Warren, Point Danger, Eastern Australia.—*Strange.*

SUB-ORDER II.—ECTOPHTHALMA. *Pfeiffer.*

Mon. Pneum. Viv., 1852, p 14. *Suppl. prim.* 1858, p. 14. *Suppl. Sec.*, 1865, p. 13.

Eyes placed at the external base of the tentacles; foot sub-elongated. Operculum horny or testaceous, distinctly spiral or not spiral, not concentrically striated. The two families, *Cyclostomacea* and *Helicinacea*, are distinguished from each other by this last character.

Fam. I.—CYCLOSTOMACEA. *Pfeiffer.*

Mon. Pneum. Viv., 1852, p. 14. *Suppl. prim.*, 1858, p. 14. *Suppl. Sec.*, 1865, p. 13.

Operculum distinctly spiral, testaceous, cartilaginous, or horny, with very many sub-equal whorls, or with few rapidly increasing; remaining characters according to sub-order.

Sub-fam. II.—CYCLOPHOREA. *Pfeiffer.*

Mon. Pneum. Viv., Suppl. prim, 1858, p. 38. *Suppl. Sec.* 1865, p. 58.

Operculum horny, rather thin, devoid of external testaceous covering, sub-circular, many whorled, nucleus central, shell turbinated or depressed.

Genus
CYCLOPHORUS.—Montfort.

Shell globose-turbinate, depressed or discoidal, openly umbilicated; aperture circular; peristome continuous, expanded or straight; epidermis thick. Operculum horny, thin, many whorled, more or less concave externally.

Animal with long slender pointed tentacles; foot broadly expanded, not grooved.—*Woodward.*

* C. liricinctus. * C. orbiculatus.

234. Cyclophorus liricinctus. *Reeve.* Plate XVI. Fig. 4, *copied from Reeve.*

Cyclostoma liricinctum. *Bens.*
Cyclostoma orbiculatum. *Bens., Mag. and Ann., Nat. Hist.*, 1853, p. 106.
Reeve, Conc. Icon. sp. 100 and 101.

Shell depressed, orbicular, whitish, spirally ridged, radiately striated in the furrows; spire scarcely elevated, apex obtuse, suture excavated; whorls $3\frac{1}{2}$, slightly convex, last rounded, encircled by 8 ridges; aperture sub-circular, obliquely angulated above; peristome straight, acute; umbilicus broad, perspective; operculum horny, thin, spiral.

Diameter, greatest 0·16; *least* 0·13; *height* 0·08 *of an inch.*
Habitat. Western Australia.—*Bacon.*

The preceding description is copied from the original. Reeve remarks that it is quite of a distinct type. The spiral ridges are not delicate raised lines, but strongly sculptured ridges, with the interstices flatly grooved. *Cyclostoma orbiculatum* of Benson is regarded by Reeve, who had the great advantage of comparing the original specimens, as being merely a smooth variety, which indeed might almost have been inferred from the descriptions, and I have, therefore, given that name as a synonym.

235. Cyclophorus orbiculatus. *Pfr.* Plate XVI. Fig. 5, *copied from Reeve.*
Reeve, *Conc. Icon.* sp. 101.
Cyclostoma orbiculatum. *Benson, Ann. and Mag., Nat. Hist.*, 1853, Vol. XI., p. 106.

Shell excavately umbilicated, orbicularly depressed, whitish; whorls spirally ridged, and grooved at the sutures and around the umbilicus, smooth between; aperture small, circular, lip simple.
Diameter, greatest 0·16; *least* 0·13; *height* 0·08 *of an inch.*
Habitat. Shores of Swan River, Western Australia.—*Bacon.*
Reeve, whose description of this species I have given above, doubts if this is anything more than a smooth variety of *Cyclophorus liricinctus*, as he found obvious traces of the spiral grooves and ridges, and next the suture and around the umbilicus they are more decided.

Genus
DERMATOCERA.—H. and A. Adams.

Shell globose-conical, narrowly umbilicated, not keeled; whorls rounded; aperture sub-circular; peristome reflected, shortly expanded, with distant margins, borders sometimes united by a thin callus. Operculum membranous, closely whorled, flat.

Animal with a conical horn, and protected by an epidermis on the posterior part of the foot.

* D. vitrea.

236. Dermatocera vitrea. *Lesson.* Plate XVI. Fig. 2, 2 a.
Fig. 3 *spotted variety, copied from Reeve.* M.C.
Dermatocera vitrea. *Lesson. Pfr., Mon. Pneum. Viv., Suppl. prim.,* 1858, p. 78.
Leptopoma vitreum. *Lesson. Pfr., Mon. Pneum. Viv.*, 1852, p. 101.
Leptopoma vitreum. *Lesson. Reeve, Conc. Icon.* sp. 15.
Cyclostoma vitrea. *Lesson, Voy. de la Coquille,* p. 346. Plate XIII. Fig. 6.

Shell globosely-conical, rather thin, obliquely striated, and more finely decussated with minute spiral lines, rather shining, white; spire sharply conical, apex acute; whorls 5, convex, last very large, inflated; aperture diagonal, nearly round; peristome thin, expanded, columellar margin straight, at its lower part forming an angle outwardly, margins closely approximating and joined by a thin callus, umbilicus half covered by the columella.

Diameter, greatest 0·62; *least* 0·45; *height* 0·10; *aperture* 0·30 *broad, of an inch.*

Habitat. All along the N. E. Coast of Australia and its islands, on leaves of trees and bushes.—*MacGillivray.*

Of this species, which occurs also in India, the Philippines, Java, &c., I believe the pure white variety is the only one which has yet been observed in Australia.

Sub-fam. III.—PUPINEA. *Pfeiffer.*

Pfr., Mon. Pneum. Viv., 1858. *Suppl. prim.*, p. 78. *Suppl. Sec.*, 1865, p. 86.

Operculum horny, rather thin, multi-spiral, nucleus central. Shell sub-pupæform, often irregular.

GENUS
PUPINA.—VIGNARD.

Shell pupa-shaped, for the most part covered by a smooth callus, usually polished; aperture circular; peristome simple, thickened or reflected; columellar margin divided in the middle by a transverse channel; right margin forming a second channel at its insertion. Operculum thin, membranaceous, narrow-whorled, flattish.

* P. planilabris.
* P. meridionalis.
* P. Coxi.
* P. bilinguis.
* P. Wilcoxi.
* P. robusta.
* P. ventrosa.
* P. pineticola.
* P. Thomsoni.
* P. Pfeifferi.
* P. Strangei.

237. Pupina planilabris. *Pfr.* Plate XVI. Fig 11 *natural size*, 11 a., 11 b. *much enlarged.* M.C.

Pfr., Pro. Zool. Soc., 1863, p. 526.

Pupinella Whartoni. *Cox, Catalogue of Australian Land Shells,* p. 32, 1864.

Shell widely rimately umbilicate, acuminately oblong, solid, translucent, smooth, slightly shining, very finely and closely striated, pale yellowish to reddish-horny; spire gradually tapering, obtuse at the tip, suture moderate, not margined nor enamelled; whorls 6, very slightly convex, gradually increasing, last when viewed in front equalling the rest; aperture nearly vertical, circular; peristome pale, thickened, rather widely expanded, in front frequently grooved, rendering it bilabiate, the right margin above divided by a narrow fissure, protected posteriorly by a callous lamina, columella slightly produced in the centre, where is another narrow canal, outwardly circular; um-

bilical space large, bordered below by a well marked ridge continuous with the canal, and having a hollow beyond it.
Length 0·53; *breadth* 0·26; *aperture* 0·12 *long, of an inch.*
Habitat. Miriam Vale, Port Curtis. Rockhampton, and Port Denison, Queensland.—*Cox.*
The largest and dullest Australian species, remarkable also for its broad and conspicuous umbilical fossa.

238. Pupina meridionalis. *Pfr.* Plate XVI. Fig. 7 *natural size*, 7 a., 7 b. *much magnified*, 7 c. *the operculum.* M.C.
Pfr., Pro. Zool. Soc., 1863, p. 526.
Pupinella MacGillivrayi. *Cox, Catalogue of Australian Land Shells*, 1864.
Shell imperforate, ovately-oblong, solid, translucent, shining, with extremely faint under the lens and very often obsolete lines crossing the whorls, pale reddish-horny; spire tumid and suddenly roundly tapering, apex slightly obtuse, suture slightly impressed; whorls 6, slightly convex, last more than equalling the remainder, and penultimate equal to three before it; aperture almost vertical, circular; peristome white, thickened, scarcely expanded, right margin forming a second channel at its insertion, rather wide and nearly vertical, protected by a bluntly triangular lamina, centre of columella with margin enclosing a tubular canal, cutting the lip horizontally as a narrow fissure, the tongue portion above broad and truncate.
Length 0·50; *breadth* 0·23; *aperture* 0·12 *long. of an inch.*
Habitat. Port Denison, Queensland.—*Wall.*
Like the preceding this is a large sized species, more glossy, but less so than any of the succeeding.

239. Pupina Coxi. *Morelet.* Plate XVI. Fig. 10 *natural size*, 10 a., 10 b. *much magnified.* M.C.
Morelet, in Journ. Conch., XII. 3, 1864, p. 289.
Shell broadly rimate, pupi-formed, horny, sub-diaphanous, shining, under the lens closely finely striated; spire oblongly-conical, apex rather acute; whorls 6, rather convex, last hardly striated, anteriorly flattish, obsoletely marked by wavy spiral lines, funiculated around the umbilical cleft, shortly descending; aperture circular, bicaniculated; peristome thickened, expanded, pallid, cut directly across by channels, external margin, outwardly and immediately above, superficially furrowed, the furrow becoming compressed towards the columellar margin. Operculum thin, horny, narrow whorled; nucleus concave.
Length 0·55; *breadth* 0·21 *of an inch.*
Habitat. Miriam Vale, Port Curtis, Australia.—*Blomfield.*

240. Pupina bilinguis. *Pfr.* Plate XVI. Fig. 6 *natural size*, 6 a., 6 b. *much magnified.* M.C.
Pfr., Mag. and Ann., Nat. Hist., 1851., p. 492.
Shell oblong-ovate, rather thin, polished, shining, pellucid, upper whorls closely striated, the striæ obsolete on the remainder, glassy

white, pale yellow or reddish; spire rather suddenly tapering, obtuse, suture slightly impressed, scarcely callous; whorls 6, four upper moderately convex, rest less so, last in front equalling all the others; aperture vertical, circular, continuous; peristome white or pale, thickened, briefly expanded, upper channel rather wide, ascending, in a line with the apex, inwardly bordered by a slightly curved triangular tongue, columellar channel obliquely and outwardly ascending, the lip partially surrounding its rounded outer orifice, above with a broad triangular, pointed columellar tongue.
Length 0·37; *breadth* 0·18; *aperture* 0·10 *broad, of an inch.*
Habitat. Cape York. Albany Island. Lizard Island. Restoration Island. Mount Adolphus Island, &c., N. E. Coast of Australia.—*MacGillivray.*

241. Pupina Wilcoxi. *Cox.* Plate XVI. Fig. 15 *natural size,* 15 a., 15 b. *much magnified.* M.C.
Cox, *Catalogue of Australian Land Shells,* p. 32, 1864.
Shell oblong-ovate, moderately solid, polished, shining, pellucid, smooth, sometimes very obsoletely striated above under the lens, glassy white or pale reddish-horny; spire tapering, obtuse, suture lightly impressed and slightly callous; whorls 6, uppermost moderately convex, rest less so, last whorl in front rather exceeding the rest; aperture nearly round, vertical; peristome and lingual appendages white, thickened, briefly expanded, upper canal, in the angle of the upper lip, obliquely ascending inwardly, lower canal cutting the columellar margin obliquely, protected above by a somewhat quadrate columellar tongue, roundly truncate.
Length 0·37; *breadth* 0·20; *aperture* 0·10 *broad, of an inch.*
Habitat. Clarence River, New South Wales, under and in decaying logs.—*Wilcox.* Moreton Bay.—*Bidwill.*
This highly polished beautiful species is closely allied to *P. bilinguis.* The truncation of the columellar tongue, which I find constant, is the most notable character.

242. Pupina robusta. *Cox.* Plate XVI. Fig. 13 *natural size,* 13 a., 13 b. *much magnified.* M.C.
Shell oblong-ovate, moderately solid, polished, shining, pellucid, not striated, pale yellowish or reddish-horny; spire ovately tapering, obtuse, suture thinly enamelled on two lower whorls; whorls 5 to 6, last in front more than equalling the remainder, penultimate equal to those above; aperture nearly circular, vertical, produced obliquely outwards; peristome and auricles white or pale, thickened, expanded, upper channel wide, vertical, bordered by a plate shewing a triangular front, lower channel obliquely cutting the columella much above the centre, and having a small lamella, triangular from in front.
Length 0·33; *breadth* 0·17; *aperture* 0·10 *broad, of an inch.*
Habitat. Warro, Port Curtis, Queensland.—*Blackman.*
Closely allied to *P. bilinguis,* but smaller and stouter, lip not continuous, and having the line of axis of the mouth much more oblique, and the lower canal higher upon the columella. A very young specimen,

apparently of this species, is very finely striated under the lens, but I cannot see any striæ in full grown specimens.

243. Pupina ventrosa. *Dohrn.* Plate XVI. Fig. 14 *natural size*, 14 a., 14 b. *much magnified.* M.C.
Dohrn, Pro. Zool. Pro., 1862, p. 183.

Shell ovate, rather thin, polished, shining, transparent, smooth, not striated, pale reddish-horny; spire ovately-conical, slightly obtuse, suture scarcely impressed, and on the two lower usually callous, and sometimes with a very faint streak of red; whorls 5, three uppermost, slightly convex, lower two continuous, last viewed in front much more than equalling the remainder; aperture vertical, circular; peristome slightly thickened, scarcely expanded, upper channel oblique, protected by a triangular blunt plate, columellar a little above the centre, with a triangular obtuse auricle, about equalling the other in size.

Length 0·30; *breadth* 0·17; *aperture* 0·10 *broad, of an inch.*
Habitat. Endeavour River, N. E. Australia.—*MacGillivray.*
This shell is smaller and less elongated than *P. bilinguis*, and the mouth is less oblique to the axis. Dohrn's locality, "Cape York," is a mistake.

244. Pupina pineticola. *Cox.* Plate XVI. Fig. 8 *natural size*, 8 a., 8 b. *much magnified.* M.C.
Cox, Pro. Zool. Soc., 1866, p. 375.

Shell fusiformly ovate or pupiform, rather solid, smooth, shining, in youth very finely striated, the striæ disappearing or becoming obsolete, glassy white, or pale reddish-horny; spire suddenly tapering, obtuse, lower suture enamelled; whorls 5, last viewed in front exceeding half the length of the shell, penultimate equal to last in width, and equalling in length those above it; aperture circular, slightly oblique; peristome and auricles white or pale, thickened, upper canal in a line with the apex, lamella showing in front, acute, triangular, inferior canal obliquely cutting the columella near its centre, with a short triangular plate above.

Length 0·22; *breadth* 0·11; *aperture* 0·06 *broad, of an inch.*
Habitat. Pine Mountain, Lismore, Upper Richmond River, on the ground, burrowing in dry weather.—*MacGillivray.*
The nearest allied species is *P. Pfeifferi*; but this is a larger and stouter shell, having the axis of the mouth more divergent, and very different canals.

245. Pupina Thomsoni. *Forbes.* Plate XVI. Fig. 12, 12 a., 12 b. *much magnified.* Museum, Rev. R. L. King.
Forbes, Voy. Rattlesnake, Vol. II., p. 381. Plate III. Fig. 2.

Shell ovate, solid, polished, shining, smooth, not striated, very pale reddish-horny; spire short, obtuse, suture very slightly impressed; whorls 5 to 6, last in front longer than the remainder, penultimate larger than all those above; aperture orbicular, continuous on body whorl, vertical; peristome and auricles white, much callously thickened, upper canal covered by a large curved triangular tongue, inferior larger at the lower columellar margin, formed above by the large roundly truncate termination of the columella, and below by the lip, both of which margins are prolonged upon the back of the whorl like parallel and somewhat diverging walls.

Length 0·30; *breadth* 0·16; *aperture* 0·06 *broad, of an inch.*

Habitat. Fitzroy Island, N. E. Coast of Australia.—*MacGillivray.*

This remarkable species is so unlike any other Australian *Pupina* that it need never be confounded with them.

246. Pupina Pfeifferi. *Dohrn.* Plate XVI. Fig. 9 *natural size,* 9 a., 9 b. *much magnified.* M.C.

Dohrn, Pro. Zool. Soc., 1862, p. 183.

Shell narrowly ovate, pupiform, smooth, polished, shining, glassy, translucent, white to very pale yellowish or reddish; spire ovately-conical, obtuse; whorls 5, suture scarcely impressed, callous, sub-margined, last in front equalling ½ of length; aperture slightly diagonal, the lower margin being advanced, circular; peristome white, thickened, very slightly expanded, upper canal viewed in front with an acutely triangular tongue, lower very narrow, obliquely cutting the centre of the columella, and bordered above by a rather broad truncately rounded auricle.

Length 0·22; *breadth* 0·10; *aperture* 0·05 *broad, of an inch.*

Habitat. "Rocky Isle," off Cape Flattery. Lizard Island, and Cape York, N. E. Coast of Australia. Darnley Island, Torres Straits.—*MacGillivray.*

The smallest Australian species, which is said by Dohrn to differ from *P. Strangei,* to which it is closely allied, in the parietal lamella (acute, entering), the oblique aperture, the callous suture, &c. It may be here mentioned that after examining the opercula of all the previous species of *Pupina* I found nothing abnormal.

247. Pupina Strangei. *Pfr.*

Pfeiffer, in Pro. Zool. Soc., 1854, *causa omissa?*

Pfeiffer, in Malac. Bl., 1854, p. 90.

Shell pupæ-form, very thin, pellucid, very shining, pale **horny**; spire swollen, conical towards the top, somewhat acute; suture not callous; whorls 5½, convex, last contracted, scarcely projecting beyond the base of the axis; aperture sub-circular, bicaniculated; parietal callus slightly prominent, on both sides ending in a very small acute tooth, separated by the narrow channels from the shortly reflected, somewhat thickened peristome.

Length 0·22; *Diameter, greatest* 0·11; *aperture* 0·06 *wide, of an inch.*

Habitat. Moreton Bay, Queensland.—*Strange.*

Genus
CALLIA.—Gray.

Shell pupiform, covered with a smooth shining callus; peristome sub-continuous, straight, scarcely thickened, not intersected, columellar margin entire, above appressed, reflected, altogether closing the perforation, which is conspicuous in young shells. Operculum thin, membranous, narrow whorled.

* C. splendens.

248. Callia splendens. *Dohrn.* Plate XVII. Fig. 8 *natural size*, 8 a., 8 b. *much magnified.* M.C.
Dohrn, *Pro. Zool. Soc.*, 1862, p. 183.

Shell conically-ovate, rather thin, smooth, very glossy, pellucid, pale reddish-horny; suture impressed, narrowly margined; whorls 5, gradually increasing, slightly convex, last viewed in front more than equalling ½ of the length; aperture vertical, acutely, irregularly and slightly obliquely ovate; peristome thickened, moderately expanded all round, slightly expanded and thickened at the columella.

Length 0·28; *breadth* 0·15; *aperture* 0·11 *long, of an inch.*

Habitat. Lizard Island, N. E. Coast of Australia, among dead leaves, &c.—*MacGillivray.*

Dr. Dohrn states the operculum to be "normal," by which, I presume, he means similar to that of *C. lubria,* the only previously known species. Now, in that, both aperture and operculum are circular; here, they are ovate, and the lid is extremely thin, membraneous, and, under the microscope, exhibits no circular lines of growth whatever.

Sub-fam. VIII.—REALIEA. *Pfeiffer.*

Pfr., *Mon. Pneum. Viv., Suppl. prim.*, 1858, p. 153. *Suppl. Sec.*, 1865, p. 170.

Operculum horny, sub-oval, few whorled, nucleus eccentric.

Genus
OMPHALOTROPIS.—Pfeiffer.

Shell perforate or narrowly umbilicated, turreted ovate or globose-turbinate, carinated around the perforation; aperture ovate, oval or semi-circular; peristome simple, with distant and disjointed margins, straight or expanded. Operculum thin, horny, pauci-spiral.

* O. malleata.

249. Omphalotropis malleata. *Pfr.*
Pfr., *Mon. Pneum. Viv.*, 1865. *Suppl. Sec.*, p. 177.
Hydrocena malleata. Pfr., *Pro. Zool. Soc.*, 1854, p. 308.
Pfr., *Mon. Pneum. Viv.*, 1858. *Suppl. prim.*, p. 164.

Shell somewhat perforate, ovately-conical, irregularly marked as if hammered, variegated with flesh colour and whitish; spire conical,

acute; whorls 6, flattish, last nearly equalling the spire, ventricose, with a cord-like keel round the umbilicus; aperture slightly oblique, angularly oval, orange or yellow within; peristome somewhat callous, right margin straight, basal rather angularly produced, columellar somewhat spreading.
Length 0·27; *breadth* 0·18 *of an inch.*
Habitat. Australia.—*Pfeiffer.*
All relating to this shell, which I have not seen, has been taken from Pfeiffer.

FAM. II.—HELICINACEA. *Pfeiffer.*

Pfr., Mon. Pneum. Viv., 1852, p. 318. *Suppl. prim.,* 1858, p. 169. *Suppl. Sec.* 1865, p. 184.

Operculum without any vestige of a spire, testaceous, thick, or horny, thin (it is not possible to form a well defined family from the material of the operculum), semi-oval, or sub-triangular. For remaining characters consult sub-order II.—Ectophthalma. *Pfr.* p. 96.

SUB-FAM. II.—HELICINEA. *Pfeiffer.*

Pfr., Mon. Pneum. Viv., Suppl. Sec., 1865, p. 211.

Shell heliciform, turbinated or depressed, often carinated; aperture semi-oval, or sub-triangular. Operculum not spiral, smooth or granulated.

For the description of the animal, consult sub-order II.—Ectophthalma. *Pfr.* p. 96.

GENUS
HELICINA.—LAMARCK.

Shell heliciform, turbinate, globose or depressed, covered beneath with callus round the columella, which is rather straight and flattish; aperture triangular or semi-ovate, entire; peristome simple, straight or thickened, often spreading broadly. Operculum thin, annular, semi-ovate, membranaceous or shelly.

Animal like *Cyclophorus*; lingual teeth 3. 1. 3.—*Gray.*

* H. diversicolor. * H. Draytonensis. * H. reticulata.
* H. Gladstonensis. * H. fulgurata. * H. Lizardensis.
* H. Yorkensis. * H. Gouldiana.

250. Helicina diversicolor. *Cox.* Plate XVII. Fig. 9 *natural size,* 9 a., 9 b. *much magnified.* M.C.
Cox, Pro. Zool. Soc., 1866.

Shell globosely-conoid, obsoletely sub-carinated, solid, above subconical, beneath depressly-convex; base whitish, gradually on the penultimate whorl tinged with violet, afterwards violet, then reddish, with the apex whitish, under the lens radiately plicately-rugose, last whorl with numerous obsolete spiral lines; spire obtuse at the apex; whorls 5, flatly slightly convex; aperture oblique, lunate; peristome white, slightly thickened, very briefly expanded, columellar junction below somewhat angularly rounded. Operculum reddish-horny.

Diameter, greatest 0·23; *least* 0·20; *height* 0·20 *of an inch.*

Habitat. Brisbane, Ipswich, and Pine Mountain, Queensland.—*Masters* and *Brazier.* Pine Mountain, Lismore, Richmond River, on leaves and trunks of trees.—*MacGillivray.*

Closely allied to *H. Draytonensis.* A variable shell in colour; it frequently has a dead and chalky, instead of a porcellaneous, appearance, and the red and violet of the spire are sometimes greenish, or bluish, or altogether wanting; the throat is occasionally reddish or yellowish, instead of white. My Queensland specimens are not generally so brightly coloured as a series from the Richmond.

251. Helicina Draytonensis. *Pfr.* Plate XVII. Fig. 13 *natural size,* 13 a., 13 b. *much magnified.* M.C.

Pfr., Pro. Zool. Soc., 1856, p. 393. *Mon. Pneum. Viv.,* 1853. *Suppl. prim.,* p. 207.

Shell conoid, rather solid, rugosely striated, and marked with some spiral striæ, slightly shining, flesh coloured; spire conoid, apex rather pointed, yellow; whorls 4½, rather flattened, last somewhat keeled, base more convex, with thin callus drawn over it somewhat diffusely; aperture diagonal, triangularly semi-oval; peristome white, shortly expanded, basal margin slightly arched, angularly joined with the short, simple, columella; operculum fulvous horny.

Diameter, greatest 0·25; *least* 0·18; *height* 0·14 *of an inch.*

Habitat. Drayton Range, Queensland.—*Stutchbury.*

Although I have two specimens sent me by Cuming under this name, and they agree with the description, yet I have preferred to give Pfeiffer's account, merely adding the colour of the operculum, which is present in one of the two.

252. Helicina reticulata. *Pfr.* Plate XVII. Fig. 14 *natural size,* 14 a., 14 b. *much magnified.* M.C.

Pfr., Pro. Zool. Soc., 1862, p. 277.

Shell trochiform, rather solid, thickly spirally grooved and ridged, crossed by fainter markings and lines of growth, flesh coloured, irregularly marked with blotches, spots, streaks of red or yellow; spire conoid, rather mamillary at the apex; whorls 4, flattened, last indistinctly sub-angular at the periphery, base with thin granulated callus, partially bounded by a groove; aperture very oblique, somewhat triangular; peristome very slightly thickened and expanded, white, angular above, roundly produced in front and rounded below; operculum dark chestnut, with a pale nucleus.

Diameter, greatest 0·25; *least* 0·22; *height* 0·15 *of an inch.*

Habitat. Cape York, and elsewhere on the N. E. Coast of Australia.—*MacGillivray.*

253. Helicina Gladstonensis. *Cox.* Plate XVII. Fig. 11 *natural size*, 11 a., 11 b. *much magnified*, 11 c. *portion of surface.* M.C. Cox, *Catalogue of Australian Land Shells*, p. 34, 1864.

Shell depressly globular, very irregularly rugose, the corrugations often confluent, tending to run in two directions and cross each other diagonally, with some spiral lines, and others oblique, pale reddish-brown, sometimes whitish towards the mouth, mottled with white wrinkles, which look as if enamelled; spire broadly conical, obtuse; whorls 5, last obscurely angulated at the base, convexly rounded for remainder; callous deposit at the base thin, granulated; aperture diagonal, triangularly semi-circular; peristome white, thickened, moderately reflected, angular above, rounded below, moderately produced in front; operculum dark, horny.
Diameter, greatest 0·15; *least* 0·13; *height* 0·10 *of an inch.*
Habitat. Gladstone, Port Curtis, Queensland.—*Blomfield.*
The smallest recorded Australian species, variable somewhat in colour, but very remarkable on account of the irregular rugæ, sometimes continuous, and forming short elevated linear wrinkles.

254. Helicina fulgurata. *Cox.* Plate XVII. Fig. 10 *natural size*, 10 a., 10 b. *much magnified.*

Shell lenticular, sharply carinate, without any spiral lines, only shewing very faintly under a lens of high power, radiating striæ, rather shining, reddish-yellow, with numerous zigzag white radiating bands; spire broadly conical, scarcely obtuse, suture margined along penultimate whorl; whorls 4½, nearly flat, last very sharply carinated, base with a circumscribed callous deposit; aperture somewhat triangular, oblique; peristome (*not perfect*) very slightly arcuate above, more so below, with an external angle, columella straight; operculum shelly, white.
Diameter, greatest 0·25; *least* 0·20; *height* 0·12 *of an inch.*
Habitat. Rocky Isle, near Cape Flattery, N. E. Australia.—*MacGillivray.*

255. Helicina Lizardensis. *Cox.* Plate XVII. Fig 12 *natural size*, 12 a., 12 b. *much magnified*, 12 c. *operculum.* M.C.

Shell between globosely-conical and trochiform, rather solid, glossy, spirally, regularly striated, with very faint radiating decussated lines, whitish, with one broad spiral yellow band; spire broadly conical, apex obtuse; whorls 5, flattened, last rounded at the periphery; base with an extensive deposit of thin granulated callus, partially circumscribed by a groove; aperture diagonal, somewhat triangular; peristome white, slightly thickened and expanded, angular above, roundly produced outwardly, and roundly joining the columella; operculum reddish-horny.
Diameter, greatest 0·25; *least* 0·23; *height* 0·21 *of an inch.*
Habitat. Lizard Island, N. E. Coast of Australia.—*MacGillivray.*
Judging from Pfeiffer's description of *H. Yorkensis* this is its nearest ally; indeed, were it not that my six specimens exactly agree with each other in sculpture, markings, &c., and have the operculum

reddish-horny instead of white, I should have been inclined to pause before describing it as a new species.

256. Helicina Yorkensis. *Pfr.* Plate XVII. Fig. 16 *natural size*, 16 a., 16 b. *much magnified*. M.C.
Pfr., Pro. Zool. Soc., 1862, p. 277. *Mon. Pneum. Viv.*, 1865. *Suppl. Sec.*, p. 228.

Shell globosely-conical, rather solid, somewhat closely spirally striated, flesh-coloured, with a sutural yellow fascia, and another broader brownish-violet band; spire regularly conoid, rather acute at the apex; whorls about 5, flattened, last a little exceeding the spire, rounded at the periphery, beneath in the centre with white, granulated circumscribed callus; columella callous, arched, not very oblique, somewhat semi-circular; peristome shortly expanded, basal margin arcuately joined with the columella; operculum whitish.

Diameter, greatest 0·22; *least* 0·20; *height* 0·17 *of an inch.*
Habitat. Cape York, N. E. Coast of Australia.—*MacGillivray.*

I copy Pfeiffer's description, not having access to any specimen having yellow and violet spiral bands, and a whitish operculum. Two specimens received from Cuming, in whose collection the type is retained, belong to two varieties of another species.

257. Helicina Gouldiana. *Forbes.* Plate XVII. Fig. 15 *natural size*, 15 a., 15 b. *much magnified.* M.C.
Forbes, Voy. of Rattlesnake, Vol. II., p. 382. Pl. III. Fig. 3.

Shell depressly-globose, rather solid, slightly shining, spirally striated, the striæ faintly intersected by radiating lines, colour reddish, yellowish, or brownish; spire broadly conoid, obtuse; whorls 5, flattened, last obscurely angulated; aperture oblique, somewhat triangularly lunate, angular above and below, with much finely granulated, thin, callosity between the margins; peristome white, thickened, shortly expanded; operculum yellowish-horny.

Diameter, greatest 0·23; *least* 0·20; *height* 0·15 *of an inch.*
Habitat. "Two Isles," near Cape Flattery, and Lizard Island, N. E. Coast of Australia.—*MacGillivray.*

ADDITIONS.

PAGE 11. No. 25. Helix fricata. *Gould. Add* Plate XI. Fig 17, *copied from Reeve.*

,, 21. ,, 51. Helix Diemenensis. In the observations, *after* Helix coma of Gray. *Add* Plate XVII. Fig 4, *copied from Reeve.*

,, 26. ,, 66. Helix Strangei. *After* Plate XVIII. Fig 17. *Add* also Plate V. Fig 9.

,, 69. ,, 171. Bulimus Adelaidæ. *Ad. and Ang. Add* Plate XIII. Fig 5.

258. Helix vitracea. *Ferussac.* Plate XI. Fig 20, 20 a., *copied from Ferussac.*
Pfr., Mon. Hel. Viv., 1848, Vol. 1, p. 253.
Helix vitracea. *Fer. pr.* 146. *Hist. t.* 64, *F.* 5.
Shell, with the perforation covered, globulose, thin, glassy, carinated; whorls 4½, rather convex, aperture lunately elliptical; peristome simple, somewhat reflected.
Diameter, maj. 19; *min.* 16; *alt* 14 *mill.*
Habitat. New Holland.—*Beck.*

259. Vitrina aquila. *Cox.* Plate XVIII. Fig 14, 14a.
Shell globosely-auriform, opal-horny, more opaque below than above, but little shining, regularly and strongly striated with lines of growth which are decussated by very fine striæ; spire raised, papilliform; whorls 4, the last globose; suture broadly and distinctly margined; aperture oblique, ovately-rounded, margin well defined.
Diameter greatest 0·78; *least* 0·55; *height* 0·45; *aperture,* 0·48 *long,* 0·45 *broad, of an inch.*
Habitat. Eagle Scrub, near Brisbane, Queensland—*Brazier.* Under bark at the root of a tree.

260. Helix Edwardsi. *Cox.* Plate XIX. Fig. 3, 3a. M.C.
Shell solid, openly, narrowly, and deeply perforated, globose, striated by lines of growth which are everywhere closely decussated by fine transverse anastomosing wrinkles of irregular size, giving, without the aid of a lens, a wavy granular appearance, white beneath an olive-yellow epidermis, and ornamented by a broad very dark chestnut band below the suture; spire short, obtusely conoid; whorls 5, the last much the largest, inflated, descending in front; aperture

ovately-rounded, opal within, except opposite to the band, when it is of the same colour; peristome thickened, intensely black, and coarsely granulated by large round black granules easily recognised without the aid of a lens, margin reflected, columellar margin not toothed, broadly dilated and reflected, ½ covering the umbilicus, margins approached, joined by a thick black callus, spreading over that portion of the body whorl which projects into the aperture as far as can be seen, and having the same coarse granular aspect as the peristome.

Diameter, greatest 1·57; *least* 1·28; *height* 1·47 *of an inch.*
Habitat. The Liverpool River, N. Coast of Australia.—*Edwards.*

This fine species, as well as the two following, were obtained during Captain Cadell's recent expedition to the N. Coast of Australia, in large numbers, at the locality mentioned. Closely allied to and resembling *Helix pomum*, but easily distinguished from that species by its black coarsely granular aperture, by the black band which follows the suture, and by its transverse wrinkled sculptured surface.

261. Helix Creedi.   *Cox.*   Plate XIX. Fig. 2, 2a.   M.C.

Shell deeply, openly, but rather narrowly perforated, globosely depressed, finely striated by lines of growth, dull-fawn coloured, darker towards the apex of the spire, ornamented by two brown bands, one forming a fine dark margin to the suture, the second rather above the periphery; whorls 5½, convex, the last rapidly increasing in size, rather inflated, descending in front, spire slightly raised, margin broad, impressed; aperture oblique, thinly enamelled, shining and whitish within; peristome a little thickened and broadly reflected, margins somewhat approached, joined by a thin shining callus; columellar margin dilated, slightly covering the umbilicus.

Diameter, greatest 1·05; *least* 0·82; *height* 0·70 *of an inch.*
Habitat. Cadell's Straits, N. Coast of Australia.—*Dr. Creed.*

262. Helix Wesselensis.   *Cox.*   Plate XIX. Fig. 4, 4a, 4b. M.C.

Shell deeply, openly, and rather broadly umbilicated, globosely depressed, white, thin, transparent, shining, very faintly striated by lines of growth, ornamented by two orange-brown bands, one very narrow, forming a margin to the suture below, the second narrow above the periphery; whorls 5, flat above, rounded, and rather dilated below, gradually increasing in size till the last ¼ turn, when it becomes flattened on the side and narrowed, and towards the peristome sharply reflected and constricted below, forming a broad deep channel running into the umbilicus; suture deep, broad; aperture ovately rounded; peristome thin, margins much approached, unconnected by a callous deposit, right margin slightly everted, left and columellar margin broadly reflected, arching over the channel running into the umbilicus, formed by the constriction of the last whorl.

Diameter, greatest 0·83; *least* 0·65; *height* 0·40 *of an inch.*
Habitat. Wessel Islands, near the N. Coast of Australia.—*Dr. Creed.*

Plate II

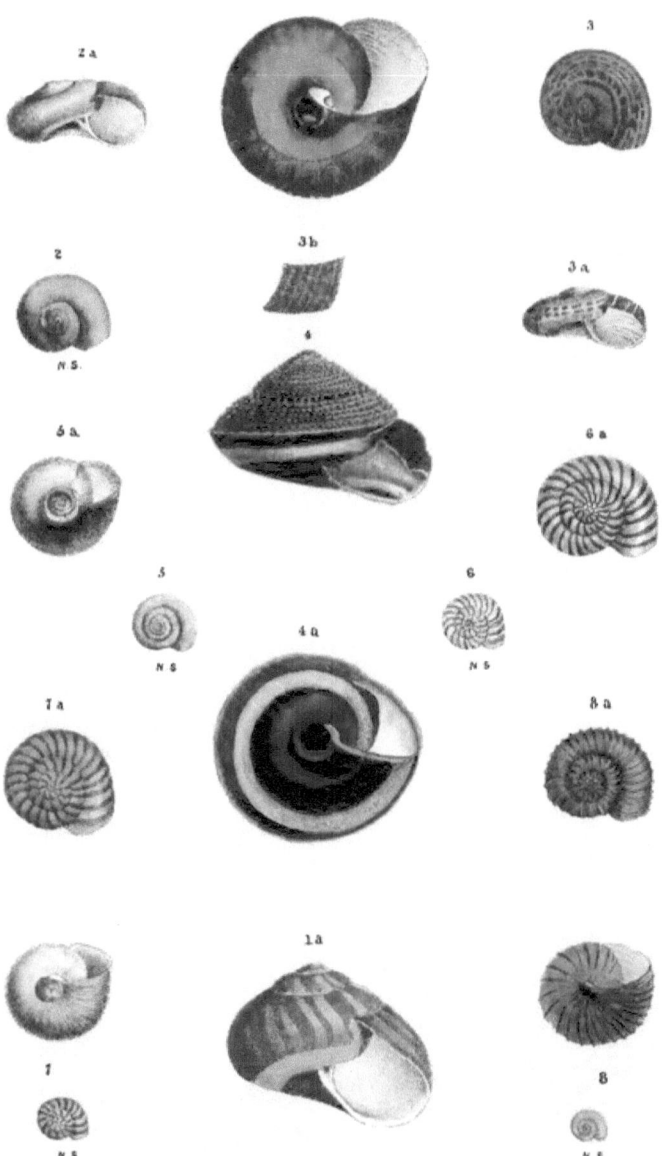

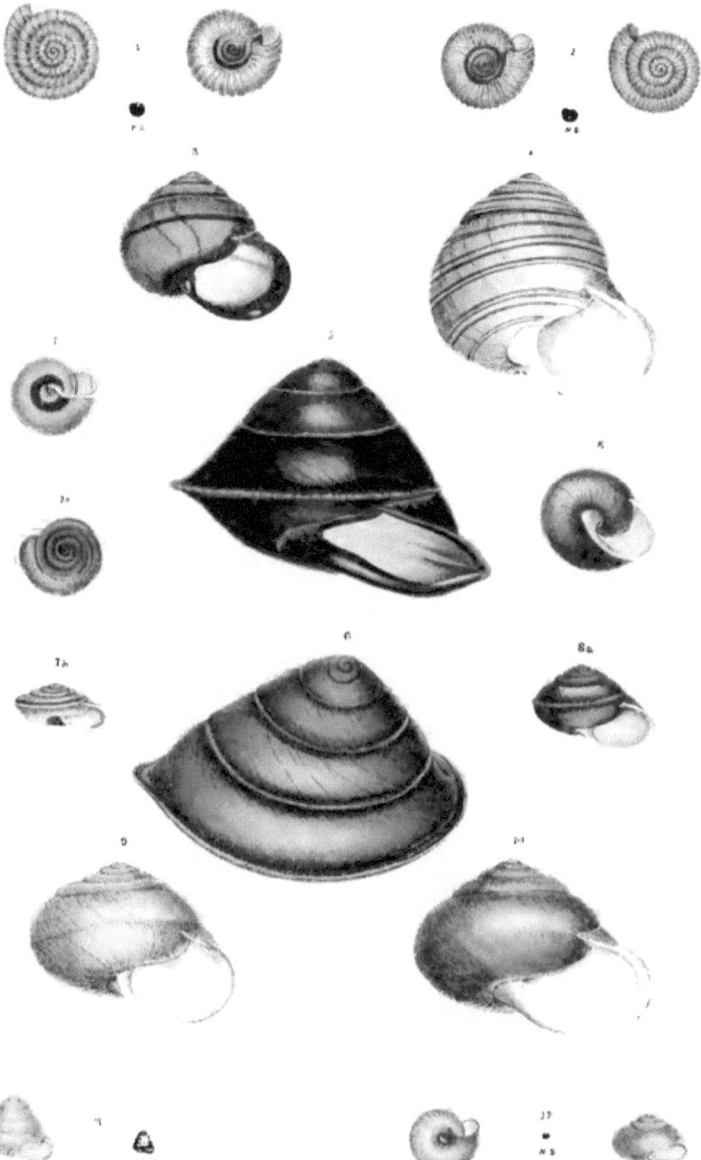

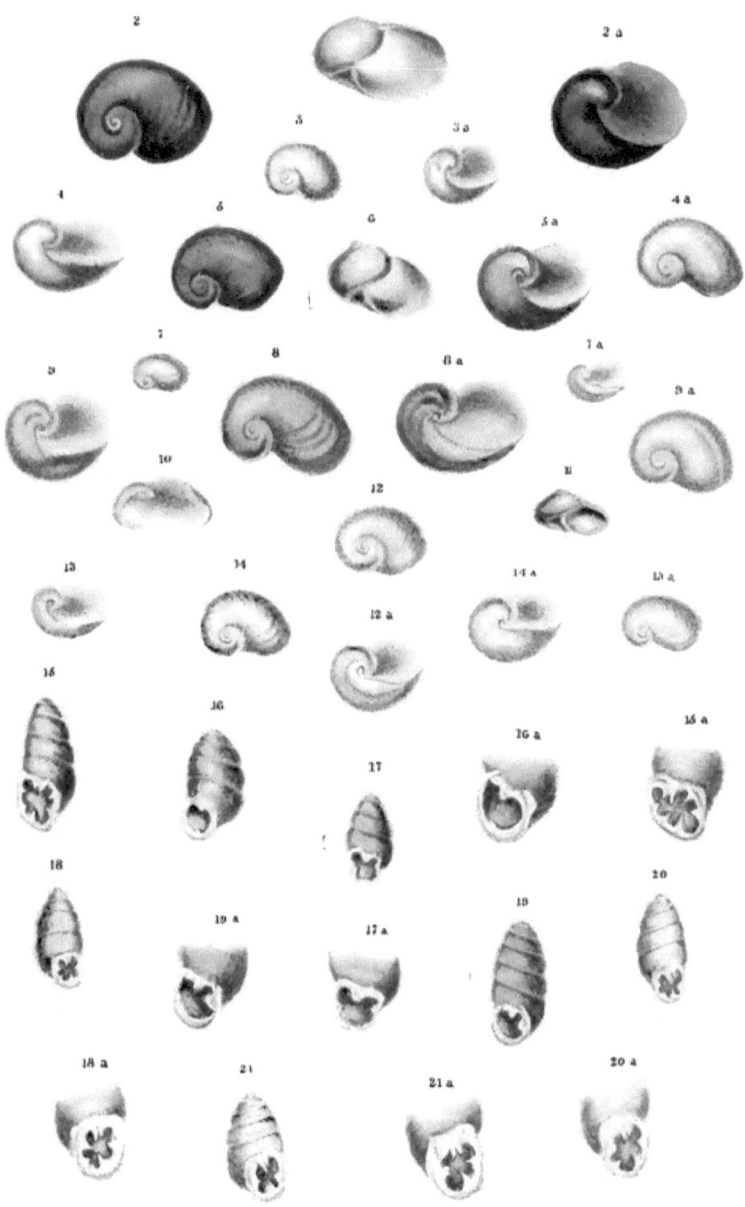

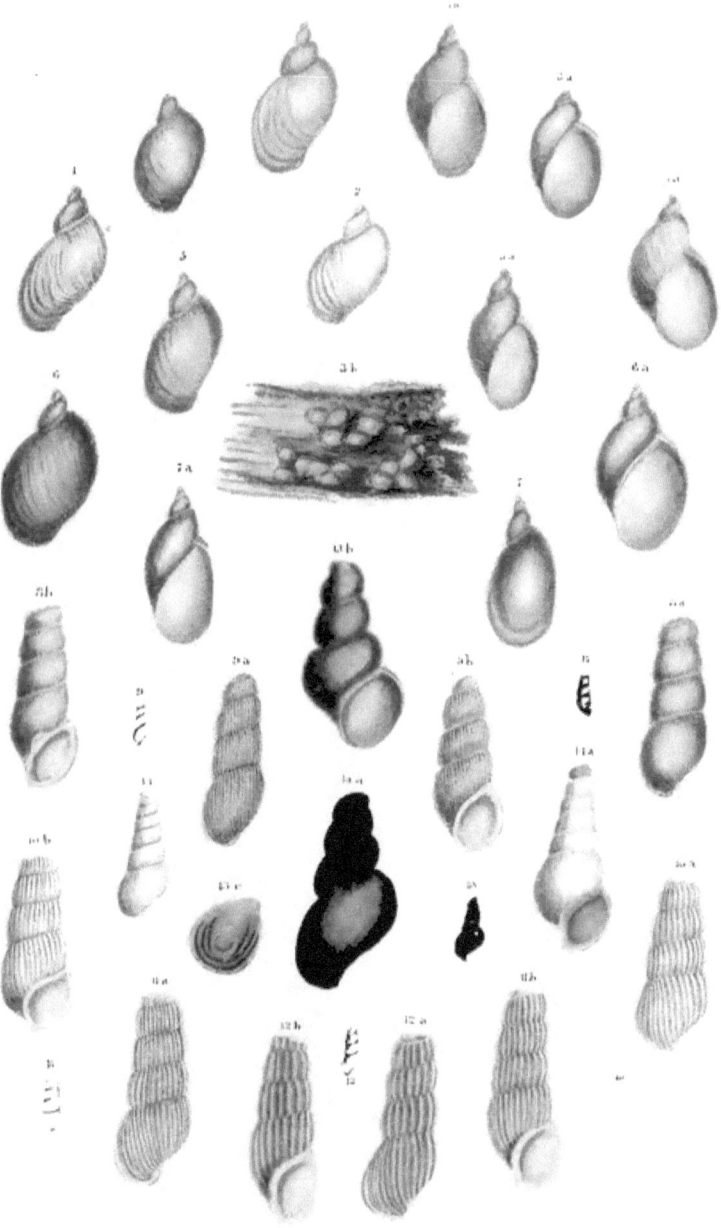

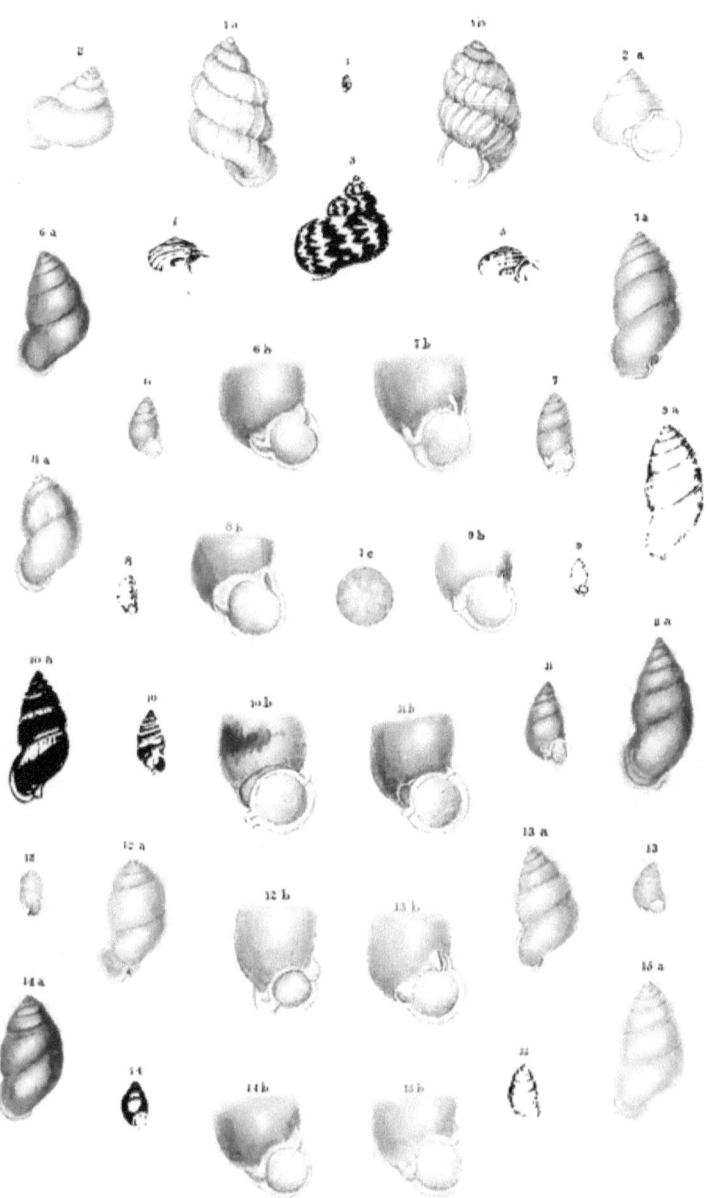

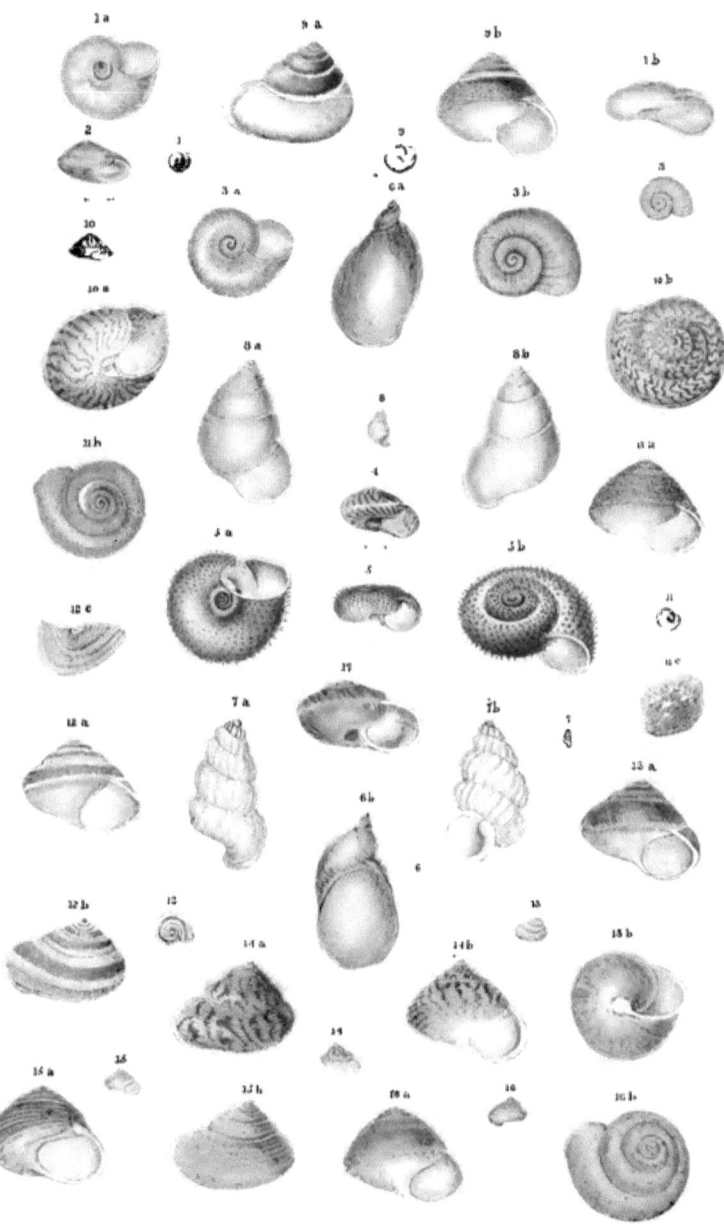

www.ingramcontent.com/pod-product-compliance
Lightning Source LLC
Chambersburg PA
CBHW030319170426
43202CB00009B/1070